GRAYSON PERRY
PORTRAIT OF THE ARTIST AS A
YOUNG GIRL

GRAYSON PERRY

Portrait of the Artist as a Young Girl

WENDY JONES

CHATTO & WINDUS
LONDON

Published by Chatto & Windus 2006

2 4 6 8 10 9 7 5 3 1

Copyright © Wendy Jones and Grayson Perry 2006

Wendy Jones and Grayson Perry have asserted their right under
the Copyright, Designs and Patents Act 1988 to be identified
as the authors of this work

First published in Great Britain in 2006 by
Chatto & Windus
Random House, 20 Vauxhall Bridge Road,
London SW1V 2SA

Random House Australia (Pty) Limited
20 Alfred Street, Milsons Point, Sydney,
New South Wales 2061, Australia

Random House New Zealand Limited
18 Poland Road, Glenfield,
Auckland 10, New Zealand

Random House South Africa (Pty) Limited
Isle of Houghton, Corner Boundary Road & Carse O'Gowrie,
Houghton, 2198, South Africa

The Random House Group Limited Reg. No. 954009
www.randomhouse.co.uk

A CIP catalogue record for this book
is available from the British Library

ISBN 0 7011 7893 0

Papers used by Random House are natural,
recyclable products made from wood grown in sustainable forests;
the manufacturing processes conform to the environmental
regulations of the country of origin

Typeset by Palimpsest Book Production Limited, Polmont, Stirlingshire
Printed and bound in Great Britain by
William Clowes Ltd, Beccles, Suffolk.

For Philippa and Flo. G.P.

For Solly, whose frequent naps made this book possible. W.J.

CONTENTS

'Eyes as big as saucers'
Hans Christian Andersen, 'The Tinder Box'

PREFACE

WENDY JONES

Grayson would arrive for the interviews, stride into the hall, take his crash helmet off in the sitting room, sit down in the kitchen and want to begin.

He was open, sometimes shockingly, sometimes hilariously, so. I don't think any subject matter bothered him, he would talk about anything, reveal anything, but he was concerned to be exact and there were many pauses on the tape where he was thinking. He was very clear on the details of his life.

One evening, six years ago, while we were sitting round his kitchen table, I had said to Grayson, 'I could do your biography,' to which he replied, 'All right, then.' It was just a spur-of-the-moment idea. We had met in 1997 through a therapy centre where his story had been one among many, no stranger than the others, only more wittily told and with the embellishment of nice dresses. He liked clothes and I liked clothes. And I liked his honesty – which made him insightful, hilarious and vital. And he was up for talking about anything. He was a lot of fun.

So the next week I turned up without a tape recorder and Grayson got his big, black, blingy ghetto blaster from upstairs and we sat in the sitting room to begin. As neither of us had a mike and as the mike on the ghetto blaster was all of a centimetre big, and not very good, Grayson had to speak with his mouth up next to it. It was all rather trying, but we felt it went well enough. A few weeks later I turned up at his cottage in Sussex, again without a tape recorder, and Grayson lugged his music centre down from London and sat bent over double, talking into the aforementioned ghetto-blaster mike, and told me the next instalment of his life. Unfortunately, the ghetto blaster failed to record and there was much 'bloody' and 'fucking' and 'pigging' from the interviewee. So I went to John Lewis and bought a cassette voice recorder.

I thought if I listened very intently, if I gave my whole attention without judgement, all would be revealed. It wasn't actually the case, but it was a noble idea. I sat in complete silence for a good many interviews until Grayson told me about the horse collar.

I wrote the book and it sat in a tin on my shelf. Then one Sunday afternoon on the train back to London he mentioned, 'I might be up for the Turner Prize this year.'

So I went home and took out the manuscript. 'You *are* going to get a digital voice recorder, aren't you?' Grayson said.

We decided to cover the first twenty-two years of Grayson's life, until he made his first plate, which marked his birth as an artist. We sat at the table and drank what Grayson called hippy tea and got on with it. Grayson arrived ten minutes early on one or other of a selection of bicycles and motorbikes, one of which looked like something that Danger Mouse rode. Although Grayson's manner was relaxed and he was a bit of a chirpy, cheeky chap, he was very disciplined, always punctual and highly focused. This was a man who, despite appearances, didn't muck around.

During the interviews Grayson appeared almost physically malleable. It seemed that sometimes he would look like a First World War pilot, then a medieval minstrel, then a housewife suffering from ennui, then an elegant hurdler. He was always morphing – I hadn't come across that before and I doubt I shall see it often again.

Hearing the same story six years later, it was clear that Grayson had become more confident. This time it was a softer telling; funnier and – although I doubt he would like it said – more forgiving. It was a past formed, fired and polished into something smooth. Once he said that it was only now he was realising how much he owed the art world, cleared his throat, went to get a drink of water, then came back and changed the subject.

Afterwards he would talk about what he had been doing, where he'd been the night before, the pot he was making, the apple-green dress he was having made for Claire to wear when she went to meet the Queen, the art student who'd turned up on the doorstep with a compilation tape – he thought Grayson might particularly like track nine as it was about masturbation. It seemed that, almost weekly, he became more successful and more demands were made upon him. It was both a delight and a strain. But this newfangled life was still peripheral to the making of his pots and the ideas he was decorating them with.

Halfway through the process Grayson read a rough draft, many thousands of words too long and said he lay awake that night thinking, 'What have I done?' I was surprised that this exhibitionist soul, so happily naked both physically and emotionally, might have reached a wall and found a space within that wasn't for revealing. There was also the gravity of revealing other people's lives. We talked about paying the advance back, letting the book go. We both understood that this was Grayson's version, that people from his past had their versions too.

The night he won the Turner Prize, Grayson, his daughter and I spent a quiet quarter of an hour wedged in a poky corner of Soho House with the party going on around us. Flo and I were trying not to sit on his dress. Grayson said 'I can't believe it' quite a lot of times and, 'I'm just trying to stay grounded.' He took the cheque out of his handbag and we looked at it and said that it was quite a lot of money, wasn't it?

Since that night I have often heard him say 'My life is like a fairy tale' and it is: a lost parent, a step-parent, chores, banishment, apprenticeship, adventures, then eventually finding himself in a dress at a ball.

PROLOGUE

GRAYSON PERRY

*'What Kind of Man Has Made
this Kind of Art?'*

'Oh the fucking, fucking, bloody, fucking, pigging . . . it's this stupid microphone, I'm going to leave it like that. I'm just going to sit here and hope that it records.'

This book is about the engine that drives me as an artist now. When people are looking at my work, I would like this book to sound as a hum in the background, the hum of my artistic engine. It is a portrait of the artist; it is what kind of man has made this kind of art.

I have been reading Hans Christian Andersen's biography: his tales are autobiographical in varied ways. I sympathise with him in that his psychology seeps out, often undiluted, often unchanged, into his fables. I thought about this recently while decorating a vase called *Internal Conflict* because I was referring to a drawing I did as a teenager. It was a black-and-white sketch of a giantess towering over a street scene. I imagine parents on the school open day were looking at the art display area and whispering, 'Look at his drawing, he's fucked up!' I see the chattering parents nudging each other and agreeing, 'The mad boy in the class!'

I

IT'S NOT UNUSUAL

The Co-op milkman was a charmer, good-looking and dark: Elvis meets Tom Jones. And Tom Jones was my mother's favourite, 'It's Not Unusual' and 'The Green, Green Grass of Home' frequently boomed out of the gramophone. The milkman was doing his round on our council estate. The first time I met him was on a cold, windy day – the front door blew open, smacking me in the head. I have a very strong memory of his silhouette against the light before being whacked and knocked over. It was a sign of things to come.

My mother danced with my father at a Broomfield Youth Club Social Evening. They dated and married in 1957 at the church in Broomfield, which is near Chelmsford in Essex, when she was twenty-one and he was twenty-three. I don't know what my mother's motivation was for marrying my father: perhaps she fell in love. My father was a decent man, when they met he would have been fresh out of the RAF, and I imagine he seemed a very capable provider. He was a keen photographer and there were pictures of them on their honeymoon in Scotland. They set up home in a council house in Acorn Crescent behind Chelmsford museum. When she got married, she immediately left her job as a solicitor's secretary to become a housewife; she could have had a career, she was intelligent, but it wasn't the done thing. I was born in St John's Hospital in Chelmsford on 24 March 1960, at ten to seven in the morning and, apparently, I was a good baby, i.e. quiet. I don't have any pictures of myself as a baby because all the photographs my father took from that time were burned by my mother or stepfather when they expelled my father's memory. I don't know a great deal about my parents because I haven't had much of an adult relationship with them; I'm unclear about their history; I only have word-of-mouth and fantasy.

In the autumn of 1964 my mother was a housewife, I was four and my sister was two. My father was working for Rayrolls engineering factory in Chelmsford and also had a part-time evening job as a wine waiter in a local dinner-dance restaurant called, appositely, the Lion and the Lamb. One night my father unexpectedly came home early and, when he turned the corner into our road, he saw the milkman's car – which was very noticeable, being a powder-blue E-type Jag – parked outside our house. He knew whose car it was and he must have put two and two together because it was late at night. Instead of challenging the man then and there, he drove back round the corner, pulled over and waited, then came home after the milkman had gone. The next morning he confronted my mother. She put her hands up in the air, proclaiming, 'Yes. I love him. And I want to live with him.'

My father upped sticks and went back to live with his mother. He returned a few weeks later although his wife was still carrying on her affair because both families were begging him to stay with her for the sake of my sister and myself. It was during the Easter holiday of 1965 that my father discovered my mother was pregnant by the milkman. The milkman had three women pregnant at the same time. He was married already – he had a wife who lived nearby – and he was having an affair with a teacher and they were both pregnant.

Surprisingly, there was no real animosity between my dad and the milkman. My father went for a drink with him over which the milkman said to him, 'I want you to bring up the child as your own.' He must have been panicking with three lots coming along at once. Perhaps he was thinking, 'If I can park one of them off with the gullible husband . . .' Maybe the milkman turned on his charm, reckoning he could persuade my father that this was a good thing, but my father wasn't having any of it.

When he found out about my mother being pregnant he'd had enough, that was it, he was gone. The evening he left, I was in my mum's and dad's bed; I used to get into bed with them, as kids do. It was a hideous, solid bed that my father had made, with a beige Formica headboard and built-in bedside tables – my mother slept in it for years afterwards. It was dark when my father came to say goodbye. He whispered, 'I'm going to go on holiday now.'

Some time afterwards my sister and I went for a day trip with our dad to Dungeness power station because he wanted to show us where he was working. I can remember exactly where we were when the question came up, so it must have struck me forcefully. We were driving past Sandon High School, it was dark and I was sitting in the back of the car when he asked, 'Do you want to live with your mother or your father? You've got to choose between me and your mother.' I remember not knowing what to say; my sister was three and I was five; we were unable to make a choice. It was an impossible bind because my mother was my mother while my father had already flown the nest and was an unknown quantity. It was too painful to consider. I mumbled, 'iwanttostaywithmymum.'

My sister and I, 1967

The wrangling over the divorce was a constant theme of my mother's conversation; my sister and I were caught in the middle of a feud. The divorce was never clearly and simply described to us, no one explained, 'This is what's happening.' Perhaps all parties were so ashamed of what they were doing that they didn't want to admit it to their children, perhaps it was insensitivity or perhaps they thought it was a bad idea to explain the affair plainly to the kids, so it was all very fudged in my mind. I found out most of the course of events many years later. Nobody took responsibility for us. It felt as if no one was adult enough to see what was going on.

From *Cycles of Violence*, 1992

There was an air of upheaval throughout that time. The first Christmas without my father, my mother showed me a cutting from the newspaper about my Uncle Eric's wife, Aunty Audrey, who had taken a pleasure flight at an air show at Wethersfield Air Base. When they landed, Uncle Eric wanted to take her photo in front of the twin-engined plane but she stepped back into the propeller when it was still spinning and was chopped to pieces. She had two sons.

The milkman moved in soon after Christmas and I never went into my parents' bed again. He left his wife, and the teacher, for my mother, although ironically my mother had a miscarriage, whereas the other two women went on to have babies. When my mother miscarried the doctor thought she had performed an abortion on herself, querying, 'What did you use, a knitting needle?' which hurt her feelings so much that my grandmother waded in to give this doctor a piece of her mind, which was a very fierce thing. But then she got pregnant by him again and my half-brother was born at home in September 1967. My brother, Neil, appeared and he was the golden boy. They weren't married, but in my mind my brother's birth cemented their relationship. The milkman was twenty-seven, four years younger than her; maybe she wanted to be with him because of his patina of glamour. He was attractive in a brutal, brooding way. He was dangerous, he was flashy and he drove a flash car – a poor man's Tom Jones. It was a relative glamour, I suppose.

When I was seven I spent Christmas with my father and his new wife in their small terraced house in Chelmsford and we watched *Thunderbirds* together. I got a pea-green Thunderbird 2 model for my Christmas present. I remember eating bacon and tomatoes for lunch, and the taste of tinned tomatoes. He kept in sporadic contact for a few years, but then he did what many men did at that time, and still do: he lost contact with his children. Fathers for Justice are a tiny minority. There should be another group with a much larger membership called Fathers for an Easy Life. When parents say it's too upsetting for the children to maintain contact, I think they mean it's too upsetting for the parents. My father made the decision not to see my sister and me any more. Seeing us meant dealing with a wound that he couldn't face attending to, so he let it fester rather than intervening and keeping the relationship alive. Instead, he left us. My dad became a ghost then. When he left, I felt bereft. The rug was pulled out from under me. As far as I'm aware, it is the event that has had the largest impact on me in my life. Emotionally I went numb, I closed down. And that's when I handed everything over to Alan Measles.

My stepfather was soon showing his real colours. My first and only nosebleed was from being whacked round the back of the head by him when I was six. We were sitting at the kitchen table and I watched the red splats of blood fall from my nose and clash luminously with the orange and white checked tablecloth. I didn't know why he hit me, what reason is there to hit a kid round the head? In subsequent violence my mother would implore, 'Not the head! Not the head!'

2

I ABSOLUTELY COULDN'T COUNTENANCE HIM LOSING

My mother's potty training technique, which worked, was to plonk me on the potty with the instruction, 'Don't get up until you've done one,' so I sat there for hours playing with my toy cars along the edge of the sofa. I enjoyed being on the potty so much I didn't want to get off, so I shuffled around the garden on it until the base eventually wore out. When I did learn to use the toilet, at first I would sit on it back to front facing the cistern so that I could play with Lego and toy cars on the cistern lid. Years later when my stepfather burst in on me once while I was leaning over playing with a racing car on the mat in front of the lavatory, he snorted disparagingly, 'Bloody ridiculous!' because I was twelve by then. It was while I was on the toilet that I first began making my imaginary world.

The focal point of my imaginary realm was my teddy bear. Alan Measles was bought for me for my first Christmas when I was nine months old. He was a yellow teddy bear, about ten inches tall, with little black bead eyes; a cheap one, not a posh nor particularly flash one, just a workaday lump of foam, but he did the job. One day he got too close to the fire and his ear burned off so the neighbour knitted a new ear. He wore an orange boiler suit that my Aunty Mary knitted for him. He is thin now because he was loved to bits. He's the only artefact I have left from my childhood.

My first memory is of meeting the boy next door, Alan Barford, who was slightly older than me, through the fence on the front lawn. I can also vaguely remember having measles when I was three and looking out of the window and seeing deep snow – it was the severe winter of 1963. I had to spend a lot of time in bed and my teddy and I bonded at that point. He became Alan because Alan was my next-door neighbour and Measles because I had the measles, and that's what I called him, Alan Measles.

Alan Measles was the leader, the benign dictator, of my made-up land, the glamorous, raffish, effortlessly handsome, commanding character. He was supreme. My aunty knitted me a woolly tortoise stuffed with cardboard to keep its shape, so Tortoise was appointed Alan Measles's second in command: the reliable, slightly portly deputy, like John Prescott to Tony Blair.

Between the ages of five and fifteen my imaginary world solidified and its rules were drawn up in my mind. This world consisted of four islands in the Atlantic Ocean. My favourite number was four because cars – with which I was obsessed – have four wheels; so many things in Alan Measles's kingdom came in fours or multiples of four. The fish-shaped island across the top was Shark Island which, like Russia, was cold. Round Island in the south was

Alan Measles on his throne

mountainous, while Elfin Island to the east was an empty desert island. Alan Measles lived on Tree Island, which was European, forested and homely. It contained the secret valley – my bedroom – where Alan Measles hid with his army. Rebels always live in valleys. My bedroom walls were the cliff faces, my shelf was the ledge on the side of the valley where aeroplanes took off and my bed was the field. Alan Measles's army camped on my candlewick bedspread – I imagined the tufts were hedges – while Alan lived in an underground house with his six children. Like James Bond, his wife had been killed in a car crash.

When I was about ten, I worked out the game was set one hundred years in the future in the 2060s and 2070s.

There had been a calamitous nuclear war, almost obliterating Planet Earth. Everyone agreed that technology had advanced too far, so an international agreement was forged stating that from now on technology could only move backwards. Armies once again began to use old-fashioned, conventional weapons. It was my rationalisation of how I could use all the Airfix models I was now making, my First and Second World War planes alongside my contemporary jets – which came from different eras – in the same war.

One of my roles in this world was as the designer, engineer and manufacturer for Kenilworth's, the factory that assembled every artefact in the kingdom. Alan Measles would command, 'We must have a really big airliner and four bombers,' which I would then make. I had been given a basic set of Lego, enough to build a house, when I was four and had started collecting it. Using my Lego, I constructed elaborate models of cars, guns, bikes, ships and cranes. I devised an entire system for making an aeroplane, constructing it, not one Lego brick on top of another but one next to another, so it was like a tower on its side. The plane had a sleeker look when I built it sideways and, because it didn't have studs along the top, the roof slopes were aerodynamic. The Holy Grail for me was when I was building a Lego aeroplane with a retracting undercarriage or bomb bays, which I was able to do with a struggle after I'd spent hours puzzling out how to adapt the doors and hinges. I was born too early because Lego was still very simple when I was a young child. When my brother was small, he had Lego Technic that included mechanical gismos to make working engines.

Making things with Lego was a restful, almost meditative, creativity that involved solving technical problems that had no sentimental content. It was an escape from emotional chaos. There were only a limited number of options for how Lego bricks could fit together and that was comforting. I recently made a pot called *Assembling a Motorcycle from Memory* about how a large number

Assembling a Motorcycle from Memory, 2004

18

of men are at peace with life taking a motorbike engine to bits, because a motorbike engine is finite. It doesn't have the infinite possibilities and muddle of relationships.

As well as being a manufacturer I was also the reporter who narrated Alan Measles's exploits, particularly 'The Grand Rally', to an audience of children: '*Alan* got in the aeroplane, took off and was *pursued* by the Germans!' The Grand Rally was a sixteen-day annual car race that zoomed around all four islands, during which Alan Measles would have elaborate adventures and spectacular crashes in his racing car. But he would always win in the end. I absolutely couldn't countenance him losing. As long as Alan Measles won the race then something in me, some spirit, would carry on. As well as racing, Alan Measles was also shot down countless times in battle but he was *never* killed. Other characters, me included, were dispensable, easily slain and could certainly lose a car race, but Alan Measles had to be perfect, with perfect morals. Alan Measles was the ultimate male presence.

The Germans were the enemy and the invading force, or they were as soon as my stepfather appeared on the scene. Gradually, the Germans occupied Alan Measles's realm. As the years passed, Alan became more of an underground guerrilla, more of a spy. In the beginning there had been open warfare, whereas towards the end it was subterfuge. I was the guerrilla fighter. Guerrilla fighters are underdogs battling against invading forces, surviving on their wits, waging a sneaky war of ambush and sabotage to undermine a more powerful enemy, which was what happened in my relationship with my stepfather. I was a stealth fighter, an underground revolutionary pitted against someone who was too dangerous to challenge. I had to be submissive; I had to suppress my power. As I was growing up I progressively bestowed all my noble masculine traits of a high achiever, a winner, a lover even, on to my teddy bear for safekeeping. He was the guardian, the custodian of these qualities. To keep Alan Measles safe, to ensure that he was protected, I adopted the role of his bodyguard.

I lived in Alan Measles's realm, carrying it around with me like a comfy sleeping bag I could pop into at any time. I held my make-believe world in my head, returning into it to find ready-formed landscapes, narratives and relationships. If I couldn't fall asleep I imagined I was on a mission, camping on a precarious overhang on a rocky cliff or flying a spy balloon high over enemy territory. As I grew older my illusory land became progressively enlarged and embellished, incorporating toy cars, Lego, playing outside, drawing, then later on Airfix models and eventually dressing up. I no longer had separate games, they were all facets of the one game: everything was linked to this domain where Alan Measles was a major player.

I was still playing the game enthusiastically until I was fifteen. Then one day some of my brother's toy cars were lying around in the lounge, I tried to play with them but I couldn't, I'd lost the ability. I wondered, 'Is this what it's like being an adult?'

3

UTILITY MAN

When my father still lived with us I often used to stand alongside him in the shed. The shed was a square brick extension to the back of the house; it had a window with a bench and drawers in front of it that my father had made. The drawers were painted white, a very thin-looking white, each one having a different knob on it that my father had salvaged from pieces of furniture, to identify its contents. There was a red knob, a glass knob, a steel knob, a little loop knob. Everything, everything had its place. There were drawers full of brass screws like little maggots, or connector blocks like Lego bricks. My father used to comment, 'The man who invented Lego must have got the idea from electrical connector blocks because they look just like Lego, don't they?' The shed meant my dad and me, just the two of us, together.

My father tested out all the paints for decorating on the shed wall. There was a large square where he had painted up-and-down stripes to get the paint off the brush or to test out a colour to see if it was the one he wanted.

Those particular colours he chose I think of as wine gum colours: black, burnt orange, lemony yellow, bottle-green and a slightly winy red, and I have an affection for them because of the square of brush strokes. He'd painted a fifties Lloyd Loom chair in eau-de-Nil so there was pale-green on the wall too. I can remember standing by the bench, looking over my shoulder at the light streaming in through the shed door and being reflected off the patch of paint on the wall, this abstract painting on the wall, which was the first time I remember seeing a painting, or the idea of painting, as being something I might want to look at. I had no notion of art; the only picture we had in the house was a print of a tea clipper sailing ship that we got free with washing powder. We might have had *The Laughing Cavalier* too, that we got in the same way. The next-door neighbours had a coffee table with a poster of a bullfight under a glass top, with a gold plastic rim round the edge, set on these conical black wooden legs, and that seemed exotic. I think they'd been to Spain on holiday.

Some of the tools in my dad's shed were very distinctive because he'd made them himself. When he was unable to find a screwdriver that he could use with both hands, he put together an extra long one with a carved handle measuring nine inches. He always carried his own toolkit on jobs when he was working on pylons and huge electrical sub-stations. It went back to an era when a man was desperate if he had to put his toolbox in the pawn shop, as in the old nursery rhyme: 'Half a pound of tuppenny rice, half a pound of treacle, up and down the City Road, pop goes the weasel!' 'Pop' was pawning; a weasel was a pressing iron for tailoring. Pop goes the weasel was hocking your weasel down the City Road, where there were pleasure gardens with gambling and people spending. It was a sign of a spendthrift to hock the tools of your work. Even now, when the bailiffs come, they're still not allowed to take the tools of someone's livelihood. My dad's tools were precious to him and he had a lot of them, one for every job. The only possessions he came back to pick up after he'd left were his tools; that meant he had *definitely* gone.

My dad's shed was dark and within it there was the feeling of all the possibilities, all the options that were open to me; it was like sitting at a vast organ and being able to pull all the stops. Anything could be made with his tools, which was an exhilarating thought. The shed was arranged delightfully with the window in the middle and all the drawers, shelves and tools down the sides and underneath. It was like an altar. I've thought later that as a physical template it was very satisfying, as well as being a powerful metaphor for creative thought. My own creativity and art practice has been a mental shed – a sanctuary as well as a place of action – where I have retreated to make things. It gives me a sense of security in a safe, enclosed space while I look out of the window on to the world. The shed was where I first learned how to make things, where my subconscious was schooled in colour, texture and the concept of making. I still have that excitement now, of being very glad that I'm a maker and that my internal shed is always available. I can retreat into my head while in bed or in the bath – wherever I am – to think about things I want to make, and knowing that I will create at least some of them is extremely exciting.

My father could make or mend anything. He could install central heating. He could wire a house, build a brick wall or make a chair. At one point he even made his own stereo. I always imagined that if he'd had long enough, he probably could have made a car. My father and Uncle Arthur came from an era – I remember watching something about it on *Tomorrow's World* once – when men could mend every appliance in the house. Many of my uncles on my mother's side were skilled manual workers, what I call Utility Men. They did an apprenticeship and learned how to engineer things. They worked with metal, pipes, instruments and lathes. They had skills. They were industrial craftsmen. They were breadwinners. We needed Utility Men then. Nowadays most engineering is performed by robots; if you think of, say, the engineering to construct computers – no one person could make a computer because it isn't made with a file and screwdriver, whereas my father's job often involved remaking a machine part by hand. He would look at the diagram for it, saw a bar of metal into the right shape, put it on the lathe and file it. It didn't daunt him.

When I was four my father won a sandcastle competition for me while we were on a chalet holiday in Margate. He dug a hole in the sand to form a dungeon, with steps leading down to cells. It was a conceptual sandcastle. There was something bloody-minded about his approach that encapsulated my father: 'I'm going to make a different sandcastle. I'm going to make a hole. I'm not going to go up; I'm going to go down!' I went to collect the prize for Best Sandcastle in Dean's Holiday Camp and got something in red plastic. I don't remember what it was but I do remember the colour. Then I ate too many straw-berries and cream, and was violently sick in the car on the way home.

One very clear image I have is of my father bringing home a ball-bearing for me when he was working in Hoffman's ball-bearing factory. It seemed gigantic, like a cannon ball, though it was probably only the size of a golf ball. It was heavy, shiny and perfect. My dad told me that they made ball-bearings by dropping blobs of molten metal through the air into cold water and, while in mid air, they formed into perfect spheres. My father's shed was full of objects like ball-bearings: parts of engines, fixings, lengths of metal and cogs, all of which had an element of alien perfection and wonderment. They had something magical about them because they were men's jewellery. I used to play with the ball-bearing in the back garden until one day it rolled down the concrete path and into a bunch of mint. I couldn't find it and forgot about it. Months or even years later, after my father had left, the garden was being tidied and I found it again. It was rusty, like an old cannon ball, what had once been this beautiful, shiny, perfect thing.

My dad's motorbike was an ex-service BSA, one which he bought from the army. The army used to store the bikes completely coated in oil to prevent them rusting, so the minute they were started up and began getting hot, the oil would combust. My dad said he remembered that the first time he rode his motorbike he was in a cloud of smoke and arrived home completely black. When we were little he put a sidecar on his motorbike, a black, egg-shaped one that was almost like a small caravan. It had a little door, plexiglas windows and a canvas roof that he would open in nice weather. There were two seats, one at the front, one at the back, but because my sister and I were so small at the time – she would have been one and I'd have been three – we used to sit on a plank so we could see out of the window. My dad sat on the bike wearing his goggles, while we went chugging around in

THE GLIDER-BIKE SOARED OVER THE RAILWAY CUTTING
(From *Murphy's Mad Mo'bike*)

'The Glider Bike Soars over the Railway Cutting',
from *Murphy's Mad Mo'bike*

it, stopping for ice cream, and I used to poke my head out of the canvas roof.

In the early sixties most children had tricycles – heavy iron ones with solid tyres, spoke wheels and a little tin box on the back to put stuff in, which looked like a bread bin. The boy up the road who had leukaemia – it was always whispered, 'Oh, he's *very* ill' – had a brand-new tricycle. Mine was more primitive. My dad had bought

He Came Not in Triumph, detail, 2004

27

an old one, then renovated it for me. He could do everything: he was Utility Dad. He painted it black and it had a badge in relief on the headstock that said Triumph or Raleigh, and rod brakes that squeaked. It was a perfectly serviceable trike. The trike wasn't a disappointment, the disappointment was that he buggered off, let me down and left me in the clutches of the other bloke.

I don't have many memories of my father and sometimes wonder, not that I have faked them, but that they have expanded to fill the space. I can remember fragments, like him sitting me on the tank of his motorbike and driving down the road, which was a risky thing to do with a four-year-old. It was an important four years because I absorbed a lot of him during that time and it was the longest period I spent with him. I have very few memories; they are a series of idealisations really. There must have been touch but I can't remember it.

The day after my father left I was playing in the shed pretending to fly a plane, thinking the bench was the cockpit, and the vice with the metal handle that twiddles round was the controls. I even fashioned some earphones. A shed is a male space, a male nest. It's a refuge for a man.

4

'VERY SORRY, GRAYSON'

We had two teachers in my first primary school: one was called Mrs Quick, the other Mrs Moth, 'Quick! Catch the Moth!' was our joke, and the headmaster might have been called Mr Buchanan because we used to call him Mr Cannonball. Every morning in assembly, Mr Cannonball would make the whole school count to one hundred, recite the alphabet, sing 'All Things Bright and Beautiful' and say the Lord's Prayer.

Mrs Moth had a curiously kinky ritual when it was a pupil's birthday. As the class sang 'Happy Birthday to You', she laid you face down across her lap – pretending you were a piano – then tickled you while trilling, 'DA-DA DER-DER DA-DA!' She finished by giving you a number of pretend smacks on the bottom, depending on how old you were. Mrs Moth once gave me a tiny, furry squirrel and I thought, 'She really likes me because she's given me this.' In Mrs Quick's class I was one of the teacher's pets and I often brought her bunches of flowers that I picked from our front garden, and for some reason my mum encouraged this. On Valentine's Day, shortly after my father left, my mother gave me some pennies to buy Mrs Quick a present – some chocolate, she said. I only had enough money for one of those bars that had chocolates with different centres moulded into one bar. It was in a brown paper bag on which I wrote, not very clearly, 'Be My Valentine.' I surreptitiously left it on the teacher's desk and I was *mortified* when Mrs Quick held up the chocolate and announced, 'SOMEONE'S LEFT THEIR LUNCH ON MY DESK,' because she hadn't noticed the writing. At morning break I huddled in a corner of the playground, crying; I was inconsolably upset because my Valentine's Day gift had backfired and I felt humiliated. I suppose I was in a damaged state at the time. To my eternal gratitude, and much to her credit, Mrs Quick finally saw the writing on the paper bag and recognised it as mine so, at the end of the day, she called me over and whispered 'Very sorry, Grayson' and love was restored all round.

At school, I was always embarrassed by my name because it stood out and new teachers often said it the wrong way round, calling me Perry Grayson. My mother had called me Grayson because when she was expecting me, my parents went on holiday to a bed and breakfast in Cornwall where the landlady's son, a friendly chap called Grayson, showed them around the area. My mother liked him and she liked his name. It's a very uncommon Christian name – occasionally I have heard of another Grayson although I've never met one. It means 'bailiff's son'. A highly unusual name was self-defining; even at the offset I felt different.

Most afternoons on the way home from school I played in the cornfield along the back of my house. When I was five, the corn was taller than me so I trampled tracks into it, much to the farmer's annoyance, to make mazes. I was disappointed when I grew taller and the corn was no longer higher than me. The cornfield was transformed into a colossal construction area in 1966 when I was six because the North Sea Gas pipeline came straight through the middle of it and that summer the building site became our playground. We used to clamber on caterpillar tractors, and over and through precarious piles of cast-iron pipes – if they'd rolled, squash! The workmen sometimes let us ride up and down the field in their diggers and I would sit in the cabin of a JCB as pleased as punch. The tall cranes, the deep pits and the welding of huge pipes were very exciting to a young boy.

If I wasn't outside playing, I used to spend a lot of time indoors drawing. Every week I cut all the dolls from the back of my sister's *Bunty* comic, then made them new clothes. My stepfather, when he moved in with us, had brought with him a large roll of thin, light-blue paper that old-fashioned airmail envelopes were made from. On Saturday mornings my mother would give Alan Barford and me a sheet of paper and a pencil each, asserting, 'You're only getting one piece!' It would be a sizeable sheet, about A3, so I folded my piece of paper into eighths to make eight small rectangles, then I drew on each one and that gave me eight goes at drawing aeroplane battles with tiny dots for guns firing off. I drew a lot of jets because my only ambition at primary school was to be a jet pilot.

Look Mum, I'm a Jet Pilot, 2000

During that first summer holiday after my father left I
watched a children's television programme that demon-
strated how to make a hand puppet from a sock. I
rummaged around and uncovered a white baby bootee,
made the puppet, drew eyes on it and immediately felt

very fond of it because it was a toy, a character, and it was made of a sensual material – it had a woolly upper and a vinyl sole as bootees sometimes do. It was feminine and babyish. The sensation of this friendly toy around my fingers, the comfort of having my hand inside the bootee and the joy of being creative, were the first inklings of the fetishism that was to play a large part in my growing up. Only a few days later I had the puppet in my pocket while I was playing in a stream with Alan Barford and it fell into the water and got sopping wet, so I hung it on a fence to dry while we finished erecting our dam. I was upset when I realised, back at home, that I had left it hanging there: that the little puppet was alone on the barbed wire, quivering in the wind, cold and abandoned. It distressed me to think that I had left my poor, cuddly little toy to its fate in the horrible wide world. I had forsaken it and all I'd invested in it – that dismayed me; I cried in bed at night. I can't remember crying over my father leaving but I can remember crying about my abandoned toy.

5

A CURRANT BUN

Aunty Mary was definitely a currant bun and not a horse. There was a yuppie pub game in the eighties where you waited until someone walked into the pub, then everyone would shout, 'Horse!' – horse isn't an insult – or, 'Currant Bun!' There were always people who hovered around the border: 'No! No! Not a horse!' It's a fast way of dividing people into one of two. Martine McCutcheon is a currant bun and Gwyneth Paltrow is a horse. Aunty Mary was a currant bun, whereas my mother was a horse and, for as long as I can remember, Aunty Mary was a currant bun with no teeth. In those days the dentist declared, 'They're not worth doing anything with, I'll pull them out.' She had all false teeth, whereas Uncle Arthur had one tooth left and a plate that went round it.

My mother was the youngest of nine children and Aunty Mary was her older sister. She was married to Uncle Arthur and they lived down the road from my grandmother. When Uncle Arthur was courting Aunty Mary, each of her siblings had to give him a portion of their dinner when he went there for a meal because there wasn't enough food to go round. Uncle Arthur told me that my grandparents ate the meat and their nine children ate the gravy, and that when one of the children went to the toilet during a meal, they took their plate with them because if they left it on the table one of the other eight would have eaten it by the time they came back.

My Aunty Mary's house was spotless and the front lawn was mowed to within an inch of its life. She was the type of person who always did the washing on a Monday, and would hoover, sweep, clean, dust and polish the entire house every day. Aunty Mary was completely ritualistic, which I found very comforting. When she brewed a cup of tea she made it in exactly the same way every time. She warmed the teapot by resting it on the spout of the kettle so when the boiling water was poured into the pot it didn't cool down. It would always be leaf tea – never teabags – and she would wait for a particular number of minutes to let it brew so I unfailingly had a piping-hot, perfect-strength cup of tea. The tea was to go with my Marmite toast; it was a catchphrase at my aunty's house: nobody could make Marmite toast like Aunty Mary. She would do it just so. It would invariably be the right sort of fresh, crusty white bread, each slice grilled individually, buttered at exactly the right moment, spread with precisely the correct amount of Marmite, not too much because I liked a very light Marmite texture, with all the crumbs stirred up. As I finished one slice, the next piece would be waiting for me. I think that's love: love is doing someone's toast just the way they want it, on cue.

35

Aunty Mary's breakfast bowls were white and reddish-brown, and decorated with a countryside scene of a church, cottages, trees and a few cows, typical English china, but I would *not* eat my cornflakes out of those bowls. I announced, 'I don't want to eat off the pattern bowls. I want a striped bowl.' I would only eat from Aunty Mary's blue-and-white striped Cornish ware; I almost had an allergy to the patterned, transfer-printed crockery, which is ironic because I make patterned, transfer-printed ceramics now. I saw the decorated tableware as feminine and decided I was being a sissy by eating breakfast off it. Although I was only eight I would not eat out of an ornamental bowl, an ornamental bowl was girly and I was not going to go there.

At Aunty Mary's I was made to wash properly. I had a bath once a week on a Sunday, so on the other evenings Aunty Mary poured boiling water into the kitchen sink while I stood on a stool in front of her, scouring my face until it was red-raw and scrubbing under my armpits with a flannel and soap. She would be watching to see that I did every bit that was necessary, and that I brushed my teeth in the proper way and didn't cheat. And at Aunty Mary's you didn't pee in the toilet water; you peed on the side of the bowl so that people in the kitchen down below couldn't hear it. My cousin told me that.

When Aunty Mary put me to bed, I was in bondage. The sheets were pulled down so tightly over Alan Measles and me that I could barely move, but it was comforting and lovely. In the morning I'd be given a cup of tea, Aunty Mary would bring it up to me in bed, I'd read my cousin's vast collection of Superman comics and it was heaven. To stay with Aunty Mary represented a gold standard of happiness.

It was Uncle Arthur who gave me Arthur Mee's *Children's Encyclopaedia* – although the twelfth volume was mouldy because the encyclopaedias had been stacked up in Uncle Arthur's shed and as it was at the bottom of the pile it had rotted. The books, printed in the twenties when the world map was almost completely pink, were massive tomes, arranged into chapters on history, geography and poetry; there was a chapter on everything. One chapter was called 'Make and Do', with tricks such as how to peel an apple without breaking the skin or how to balance a penny on your nose. I didn't much read the writing but every photograph – and the volumes were chock-a-block with early photographs stained blue and white or rose and white – had a caption of two or three sentences which I enjoyed reading. There were countless diagrams and maps, and page upon page of illustrations of different varieties of seashells or British birds, or the internal workings of the steam engine. The most beautiful photographs were those of foreign lands when they were still very foreign: 'Log Jams in the Canadian Forest', 'Tribal Houses', or Dresden, pre-bombing when it was entirely Gothic. One chapter was called 'Wide World Wonders', with pictures of monasteries on rocks, astonishing waterfalls and tribes who dwelt in caves. There was one plate of a woman carrying a great weight on her head while the inscription proclaimed, 'Man's First Means of Transport: His Wife', which gave me an extremely old-fashioned, Imperialistic view of the rest of the world as all Wonga-Wonga Land.

37

Claire and Florence visit shrine to Essex Man, 1998

Colour pages were precious, although they only cropped up every two or three hundred pages, used to illustrate flags or a diagram of flowers that required colour. Later 1970s encyclopaedias that I read, I found slightly cheap and not very beautiful. They had a modern, easy-to-read, flashy approach in which acquiring knowledge became something you did to get a job, instead of the lovely mysterious adventure in a foreign land that learning seemed to me.

Arthur Mee's *Children's Encyclopaedias* were a comfort and an escape; I read the volumes in bed, gazing at the fuzzy images of the world. I was fond of the density of the information – the print was minuscule, the pictures compact. The quaintness and richness of these volumes affected my aesthetic, playing a symbolic part in shaping the way in which I orientated myself in the world. As they were fifty years out of date, I idealised the past, perhaps still do in certain circumstances. I was probably romanticising my own past, even by then, even by the age of seven or eight, thinking that the golden age of my life, a pseudo-1950s dream world, had passed.

There is an old picture book which I love called John Tarlton's *Essex*. John Tarlton obviously lived in Essex and took photographs of everyday life in the county from the Second World War until the seventies. One image is of a woman and her children picking potatoes. My mother and Aunty Mary would supplement their families' incomes by

In the fields, from John Tarlton, *Essex: A Community and its People in Pictures 1940–1960*

39

apple picking, planting beans or working in the fields, all back-breaking work for next to no money. I went apple picking with them once. From the book I have a warm, golden, nostalgic view of Essex with windmills turning, shire-horses plodding and nice ladies in headscarves, tatty coats and Wellington boots toiling up and down frozen fields with kiddies wrapped in Rupert Bear scarves, though the reality was probably very different, more like, 'I got one and nine pence for twenty-three hours' work.'

As well as providing me with books, Uncle Arthur gave me my first bike. I had been intensely jealous when my sister was bought a bicycle before me – although soon afterwards he came to my rescue by cobbling together a second-hand cycle. We were visiting Aunty Mary and Uncle Arthur on Christmas Day and, after we had given them their customary packets of Benson and Hedges, Uncle Arthur bellowed, 'TAR-DARRRRR!' and wheeled in a bicycle, wrapped up and tied with tinsel. The whole family was watching me. I burst into tears, charged out of the sitting room and hid in the toilet. I felt terrible because I thought I was being ungrateful, though I enjoyed riding the bike afterwards.

The bicycle had cream and rust mudguards and the previous owner had stuck model aeroplane stickers all over the frame, which I thought was very cool. It was my pride and joy – I was so happy. I taught myself to ride my bike by laying my stomach on the saddle and trailing my feet along on the pavement, then pushing off. On Boxing Day I was cycling all over Broomfield with Alan Barford when I rode over a shard of glass that caused a major blow-out of the rear tyre and it completely disintegrated. I was distraught. Uncle Arthur had to be summoned: a few days later he came to fix the tyre. I felt vulnerable because my happiness was dependent on his mechanical ability. My father was the capable mender of machines but he wasn't on the spot to repair my bike for me.

Aunty Mary and Uncle Arthur witnessed what was happening to me – it was Aunty Mary who begged my mother not to go and live in my stepfather's house because she saw how it would unfold. I knew that, compared to home, which could be chaotic and frightening, how it was at Aunty Mary's was how it should be. They knew I needed them, and having them meant I wasn't as damaged by my family as I might otherwise have been. They were salt-of-the-earth people who were kind and caring, and showed me that the world wasn't insane.

Aunty Mary's council estate, the space, the light, the little houses on little lawns, was the landscape I grew up in. It was not a landscape of slums: these were idealistically built council houses that had bathrooms and indoor toilets, semi-detached houses set in wide green avenues with blackthorn trees planted down the middle. There was a particular atmosphere of an afternoon at Aunty Mary's, of the mantelpiece clock ticking and the budgerigar cheeping and the gas fire hissing – phewww – while the afternoon faded. The twilight came through the net curtains between the two china dogs and the brass donkey, and time passed, with me lying on the floor with some Lego bricks and a toy car.

6

LIGHT-BLUE SMOCKS
FOR POTTERY

We didn't have a proper removal lorry when we moved into my stepfather's house in Bicknacre so all my mother's furniture was piled high on to a rickety coal truck. My stepfather's house was newish, unremarkable and typical of the late sixties, and Bicknacre was ten miles south-east of Chelmsford in the middle of a flat, inconsequential part of the Essex countryside. At that time it had Britain's only leper hospital and I used occasionally to see people with lumpy, bumpy faces and hands in the village shop. Once I went to the hospital fête and Ed Stewpot, the Radio One DJ, came to open it.

I was moving into a modern world. In hindsight I see Broomfield as quaint, old, fifties England, pre-consumerism, pre mass ownership of cars, whereas after the age of eight there was something bright and go-ahead-ish about the architecture around me. The same contrast characterises the metaphors I've drawn for my childhood: when I think of my father I imagine plough horses, traction engines, thatched cottages and vicars on bicycles,

Refugees from Childhood, 2001

whereas my stepfather is bleak flats and the tinny modernity of that time.

My stepfather's house was called Thorn House because it was opposite a forty-acre wood called Thorn Wood. Curiously, I always found it an unsatisfying and slightly malevolent copse as it was full of thin, brittle, nearly dead trees amazingly infested with ants. There were parts of

43

the wood where the ants' nests were teeming mounds three feet high; one of them even had a moat dug by the insects. I couldn't sit or climb anywhere because there were ants everywhere and it was the sh-sh-sh of ants that gave the wood its distinctive character.

I was enrolled in the local school, Woodham Ferres C of E, assessed as soon as I arrived ('Read this book!'), then, despite being too young for it, I was plonked in the top class, where I remained for the next three years. It was a tiny school with only sixty pupils in three classes. The headmaster, Mr Wiseman, was God-fearing and strict – he used the ruler on the palm of your hand for punishment. It was a very religious school: first thing every morning we stood in the gym and sang a hymn from a king-sized hymn sheet, like a giant flap-over notebook, that hung by a rope from the ceiling.

The first year the Christmas play was the Nativity, in which I was one of the wise men. The following year, when I was ten, we performed *A Christmas Carol* and, being a bright boy who had a memory, I was chosen to play Scrooge. It was a lavish production for a school play with changing sets, elaborate costumes and a specially built stage, made from the gym apparatus and those wooden boxes that all school halls seem to have. Even the blackout blinds were taken down to be turned into the stage curtain. We designed cardboard top hats in art and, as Scrooge, I was given a grey-haired wig to wear. One of the dinner ladies made it by threading silvery string through a skullcap, then brushing it out so it fluffed into big hair. I had to wear the wig in the dress rehearsal to get used to it. There I was on the stage, waiting for the curtain to rise, but because everything was so clumsily made, the curtain rings had been left on the bottom of the stage curtain so as it rose, the curtain rings hooked on to my wig, which was stuck on to my own hair with double-sided sticky tape, and pulled the wig off. Everybody *burst* out laughing – because I was in front of the whole school – and I was gasping, 'Ah! Er! Er! Ah!' As the curtain went further and further up my wig was being pulled higher and higher, and I was supremely embarrassed.

At the moment in the play when the Ghost of Christmas Future came, I was in bed wearing a nightshirt and long johns. As no one could find any long johns that would fit me and because the costumes were thrown together from old sheets and old clothes that parents brought in – bodge, bodge, bodge – they had made me long johns by cutting the sleeves off a white sweatshirt which were held up by two elastic garters underneath the nightshirt. On the night of the play I lost the elastic garters, got up in one scene and my stockings fell down. I was mortified. It was the most embarrassing thing I could imagine because I was on the cusp of awareness of my body and of my sexuality starting to develop.

I've got a feeling I was chosen to play Scrooge because I was the worst actor. I was able to learn the lines but I can't remember doing any kind of acting. When the teacher said, 'Can you act as if you're sad?' I'd mumble robotically, 'Ohhh Nooooooo! She's deeeeaaaaad!' so I'm not sure I was very good. I can't remember emoting very much.

The following year the Christmas play was an updated

version of the Nativity in which I was Gabriel. In this version – it being an evangelical, modern Christian one – Gabriel was the lead. I thought, 'Gabriel! Yeah . . . I can be an angel.' At playtime I ran around the field pretending to be an angel. The school secretary sewed my costume and when she measured my height and my arm span she exclaimed, 'Oh! How delightful! A square boy!' One of my earliest stirrings around clothes was over the costume which was a robe made from a white bed sheet with ribbon ties and silver cardboard wings and a halo. One morning I saw all the costumes hanging up on a line in the school hall awaiting the start of the performance and I got a little feeling I still get now when I look inside a woman's wardrobe or think about women's clothes, a little flutter of excitement with fear around it. I looked at my costume, realising, 'I've got to put that on in front of everybody. I've got to wear a dress in front of everyone and be an angel.'

I can't remember any of the everyday clothes I wore as a child. Most adults can reminisce 'I had a brilliant pair of plimsolls when I was six that I adored' or 'I had a favourite pair of blue jeans', whereas I wasn't aware of having clothes at all much until I was a teenager. Clothes were to stop me getting cold. I didn't want to think about clothes getting attention. There was an incident in a shop where I screamed blue murder because I did not want a new coat, I didn't even want to try it on. Once I got used to my clothes I didn't want to replace them. On the one side of the watershed of puberty I repressed any kind of display of my inner life, after puberty I did the exact opposite. I thought boys faded into the background, girls got attention. Girls' clothes were about flaunting, they stuck out, they were elaborate, brightly coloured and impractical, whereas boys' clothes stated, 'I'm covered up and if it gets dirty it doesn't matter.'

My first pottery lesson must have been when I was eight, maybe nine years old. The vicar's wife, an old lady, came in to take pottery classes and she told us we were going to make a coil pot. I'd never done pottery before, only plasticine modelling, but not pots, not from real clay. We were taught how to make a little coil pot out of earthenware. I went through the motions in the pottery lesson; I don't think I particularly liked it, nor did I see it as the significant experience that it was. I made my very first piece of pottery for my mum, which was a sad little yellow ashtray. She didn't use it. Then I made a couple more things, a clay whale for my Aunty Mary and a small, three-legged bowl for another aunty.

We had to wear light-blue smocks for pottery. They were made of heavy, rubberised material, similar to oilcloth, had elasticated sleeves and they fastened up at the back with snappers. In my first pottery lesson I had last pick of the smocks so the one I got was tight. The classroom helper, Miss Maple, was sweet, glamorous in a secretary sort of way and always very kind to me. She had false eyelashes and looked like Dusty Springfield – I remember her having a big beehive hairdo. I got into my smock and Miss Maple snapped up the snappers at the back. The combination of Miss Maple doing up the snappers and the squeaky, smooth, unyielding, restrictive plastic garment turned me on. I was being dressed like a small child, it felt *very* humiliating.

Humiliation is one of the most powerful turn-ons for

me. What is unsatisfying about humiliation, though, is that usually it doesn't have any consequences. The consequences are only in my own head because embarrassment is a fantasy of what other people are thinking. The only consequence of dressing as Claire at the Turner Prize, for example, is whether or not I blush because I think I look stupid. If I think I look ridiculous it's horrible, although simultaneously, the disgrace is fantastic – it's a turn-on. Yet the reality of the situation is never as shameful as the fantasy, because my personality kicks in and I'm having a lovely time so I don't get the abasement I'm seeking. I don't truly want to be humiliated, I just want the fantasy.

Most people would admit that reality doesn't live up to sexual flights of fancy. Real sex is a different experience; it has a visceral here-and-now quality that can't be faked. I could fantasise about wearing a dress, and that would be exciting and I could manipulate the emotional situation in the fantasy to give me the ultimate ignominy, but the actual experience of looking at myself in a dress is different. It's similar to the distinction between a real relationship with someone and an imaginary situation. In the fantasy scenario your sex drive insists, 'Yeah! Make her scream now!' whereas if you were actually with the person and they started screaming it would be very unpleasant.

For many cross-dressers their fantasy of outward femininity only becomes a reality when they pass unnoticed. The sole attention a transvestite usually wants is the same attention a woman would get. Some trannies search out the recognition a grown woman attracts, whereas I search out the attention a girl would receive. If you dress up as a

48

From *Cycles of Violence*

woman, you dress with the hope of passing as a woman and then being treated like a woman. Dressing up as a young girl shifts the process from authentic to symbolic because it is almost impossible for a man to look convincingly like a little girl. I've only ever seen one or two cross-dressers who could pass for a girl under sixteen. I have to acknowledge that it is a ludicrous fantasy when I dress up as a little girl, yet the boundaries aren't blurred. People are more comfortable and a lot happier with me being dressed up as a child than as a woman because it is much less ambiguous: I am a bloke in a ridiculous frock and that's nice and clear. If I try to be a girl I always end up being treated like Grayson in a dress no matter what I'm wearing.

I think of my dressing up as the heraldry of my subconscious. It's a physical manifestation, an outwardly worn symbol, of what is happening within. It's also a cry for a specific type of attention. If a man puts on a little girl's dress, he wants to be treated as a little girl and handled with care. If a man wears a business suit, he wants to be treated like a businessman: with respect. I think we all dress, to a certain extent, in the way we want to be attended to. We want to be surrounded by the emotion we associate with the clothes we are wearing. Little girls don't have to do anything, or take any responsibility, they can just *be* and are worshipped for being. They are precious dollies, dressed up like cute pets: merely standing there and looking gorgeous is enough. I love it if a woman treats me like a little girl. It often happens. I take a lot of trouble for my clothes to be authentic. When a woman coos, 'Ah! What a lovely dress! Don't you look cute?' I like it.

7

'CAN I BORROW
A DRESS?'

One morning when I was seven I overheard the babysitter tell my mother, 'I went to check on Grayson last night and he'd made a noose from his pyjamas and tied them round the bedpost.' I had tethered one leg of my pyjamas round my neck and knotted the other round the headboard, then fallen asleep. The babysitter must have come upstairs, found me like that and untied me. I don't think I wanted to commit suicide – maybe I was suicidal – I don't know. It was very dangerous. That was my first sexual experience.

The first fetish story I read was about a man who went, dressed as a woman, to visit a prostitute. The prostitute strapped him to a crucifix and he had a noose tied round his neck with a stool under his feet that he stepped on and off to be able to have the experience of hanging. While he was hanging, she would inspect him every couple of minutes to see if he was still having a nice time by feeling in his frilly knickers for a hard-on, because if he'd come he would go soft, in which case it would be time to take him down. The prostitute thought he was still enjoying himself but he was dead; apparently, when you die you get an erection. The man hadn't got back up on to the little step.

Every night I played my imaginary games with Alan Measles and, within that realm, I would visit my own scenarios. My bondage games were set in a prisoner-of-war camp where I would be bound and humiliated by the prison guards. My internal voices would be very hectoring, mocking and persecuting me. 'You deserve this punishment, you are a dog, you will be treated like shit.' I used to talk out loud and openly when I was playing my games on my own in the house. The neighbour heard me once through an open window and thought I had a girlfriend around. Maybe she picked up on the sexual nature of my monologue; maybe it was the tone of my voice.

One night I stood in my bedroom in the dark while I tied pillows on to my thighs by using my pyjamas. The German guards were punishing me by forcing me to wear a female uniform because I was a spy for Alan Measles. The next morning I asked my sister, 'Can I borrow a dress?' It was an innocent request.

She replied, 'Yeah, fine,' and seemed very casual about it. A year or two earlier my sister had ballet lessons, which I was jealous of: I assumed ballet was something I would not be allowed to do. She fetched out a couple of her ballet costumes for me. After my initial request, my sister and I didn't mention it again: I must have already decided that I would keep it a secret.

In my first year at secondary school, a boy came round

to play and I suggested, 'Would you like to put on some dresses? It's really good fun, we can dress up as ladies.' When he scoffed, 'No!' I realised it wasn't something that everybody did.

My mother worked for my stepfather on a Saturday helping him with one or other of his ventures, so every Saturday afternoon my sister and I had the house to ourselves. Saturday afternoon was when I dressed up. It became a hobby. I was twelve by then. I surreptitiously cadged dresses from my sister's cupboard, though they were always too small, then acted out detailed bondage fantasies. I always got a big stiffy from playing the bondage games and I got an extra big stiffy from doing the dressing up and the bondage games simultaneously. The old man was starting to do house clearances and the garage was full of all the stuff he had cleared. I nicked all sorts of clothes out of the garage: tatty petticoats, slips and nighties, and then I would knot myself on to a chair using stockings, pyjamas, scarves and belts. I even found corsets once.

Another time I chanced upon a prim, demure dress in a distasteful Crimplene material but I loved the repulsiveness of it: my body was responding to the ghastly strangeness of the texture. It felt very feminine, like being furnished. It was the foreignness, the femininity and the feel, the scratchiness and the unyieldingness. There was something about Crimplene: it did not crease easily so it formed a carapace of femininity. I tied myself up in that. Another afternoon I discovered a box of fifteen polyester dresses, trying them all on at once, building up the layers one on top of the other until I was like a fat woman. My

53

sister came home unexpectedly while I was wobbling around the house in all these frocks; I panicked and hid in the stair cupboard until I had taken off all fifteen. I did a lot of almost getting caught because I was quite careless; part of the thrill was sneaking about and coming close to being found out. One afternoon I donned underwear, tights and a yellow dress, put my boy's gear over the top, then sneaked to the fields behind the woods where I knew I wouldn't meet anybody. I pulled off my boy's

Golden Ghosts, 2001

clothes, stuffed them under a hedge then set off for a walk as a girl. It was the first time I had dressed up and gone out of doors.

I didn't know when I was dressing or tying myself up that it was a sexual activity because I had a complete vacuum of sexual knowledge. I hadn't yet had an orgasm. I didn't receive any sex education at my primary school because it was religious, while at my secondary school we were taught reproduction from a purely biological aspect. When a pupil asked the biology teacher, 'Miss, how does the sperm get into the vagina in the first place?' she exclaimed, 'Oh, I'm *sure* you *all* know that!' I knew very little. The boys at school boasted about wanking, fucking and shagging but I wasn't sure which was which. I'd had wet dreams but when I did have my first orgasm, I didn't know what was happening. I had strapped myself to the bedpost wearing a dress, becoming so excited I spontaneously ejaculated. I thought I was bleeding to death, I thought I had ruptured something, although after considering it and applying my scant knowledge, I worked it out. I consciously researched it in the library as well. Then I started to masturbate deliberately and learned how to do it.

Sometimes I would sit in my mother's Mini car where there would be a copy of *Forum* in the glove compartment. *Forum* was an erotic magazine with a slew of readers' letters detailing their fantasies about getting off on a bicycle saddle. Perhaps she deliberately left the magazine there as an indirect way of giving me some sex education. I acquired a sexual vocabulary from *Forum* because I was chatting to my mother about the letter page when

I mentioned, 'That's masturbation, isn't it?' to which she replied, 'Yes.'

Soon my fantasies morphed into a new format in which I imagined I was a German PoW in a military hospital with fractured arms and legs held in plaster casts. I laid a pillow on each arm pretending they were casts so that I was unable to move my limbs. I knew that when my mind strayed on to these storylines in bed at night I might get a stiffy. A key dimension was envisaging sympathetic visitors bringing me presents – there is always an element of caring in bondage. It was like being kept as a pet where I was controlled and yet nurtured simultaneously, both immobilised and humiliated. Being fixed in plaster was very appealing. It's a fetish called casting and Casters are people who spend their weekends hobbling around town with their legs in plaster because it turns them on; some will occasionally have a full body cast. It's related to mummification fetishes where people wrap themselves in Clingfilm – they use specialist-sized rolls of Clingfilm from bondage shops – until they are completely immobilised with only their noses poking out. I used to wind my bed sheets round my body until I was tightly bound. It was about being held: I don't remember being touched or hugged by my mum and stepfather. The two requisites for a parent are love plus boundaries: I think sex is the physical embodiment of love and bondage is the physical embodiment of boundaries. The pressure on my body from the restriction and immobilisation, then using my mind to imagine being humiliated or subjugated in cages, reminded me that I was alive.

I suspect there have been versions of fetishes since time

immemorial; that there have always been people with fetishes and either they didn't know what a fetish was, or they practised their own peculiar version in private with their mother's swimming cap and a rubber raincoat. There was a kinky magazine published in the 1940s called *Bizarre* which had DIY articles on how to build your own manacles, how to sew your own fetish boots and where to buy the best corsets. Many fetish scenarios present themselves in history and in films; Douglas Bader with his legs chopped off is a fantastic combination of Second World War pilot dogfighting and amputee-ism. *The Man in the Iron Mask, Whatever Happened to Baby Jane* and *The Avengers* were films that stimulated my erotic imagination. Today there is a comprehensive culture of fetishism; it's a huge industry. Everyone has a fetish – they might even have one for ordinary sex.

It is difficult to find a satisfying person with whom to enact a fetish. For every thousand people who like being prisoners, there is only one person who enjoys putting people in prison. There are too few sadists to go round. Certainly among men, there are more masochists than sadists. Most women who are willing to tie men up are professional. Many prostitutes specialise in S & M because it's a relatively safe market as it's non-penetrative and they only have to tether the person up in the dungeon – a lot of prostitutes have their own dungeon complete with stocks, cages and bondage equipment. There are plenty of dungeons around and about.

A fetish, in the particular sense of a technical, psychological explanation, is an object that takes the place of normal human relations. Instead of loving the woman, you love her high-heeled shoes. It is an ability of the mind to think metaphorically, to shift. If the unconscious can't get what it wants emotionally in a normal way, it will find an alternative pathway to get it. If you can't express your feminine side as a man, something decides, 'Well, you'd better dress up as a woman.' If you can't get a hug from your dad, you wrap yourself up very tightly in the bedclothes instead, though you don't equate the one with the other. It's your body's and subconscious's cry. It's a predisposition, sensitivity or an emotional vulnerability in a person and if that person is brought up in a harsh environment soon the fetish world comes along offering a solution. As a child, not for a moment did I think, 'This is because of my parents.' Until I was an adult it never occurred to me to equate my sex life with any lack in my childhood parental experiences. My body and mind only whispered, 'Oh, that's interesting, try that.' It would be a turn-on and the reward was a bit of a stiffy and a bit of a feel.

8

BIG, STODGY, SAUSAGY, SCARRED FINGERS

My stepfather's hobby was wrestling. He was not particularly tall, but he was strong and hairy in his shiny leotard
and covered in rope burns from being flung around the
ring. The old man was a member of Chelmsford Wrestling
Club; he practised through the week and wrestled in shows
at the weekend. On a Saturday we would often drive to
a local fair or fête around Essex where there'd be an hour
or two of wrestling bouts in a large white marquee that
people paid to enter. Sometimes the old man was a solo
wrestler, other times he would be in a pairing with his
friend Max, which they called the Masked Marauders. He
wore a whole-head hood with the mouth, nose and eyes
cut out, like an executioner's mask, with an 'M' on the
forehead that my mother had sewn for him. Once my stepfather hurled Max out of the ring and he landed on a boy
sitting in the front row, breaking the boy's leg. The other
act he performed was called the Man in the Iron Mask
for which he wore a catering-sized baked bean tin on his
head. A friend who worked in the local metalworking shop

turned the tin into a helmet complete with nose-piece and eye slits. He donned a black, swirling cape and he was the Baddie pretending to shout in German, so the Groundies bellowed 'Boo! Hiss!'. There were many comic incidents and lots of cheering although there was always a moment when his mask got twisted round. The Baddies always lose – I think the Baddies always lose. He was very proud of his wrestling.

The old man would launch into wrestling matches with my mother and I would be frightened because she used to implore *me* to help her. I felt I should rescue my mum when she was being throttled although it was too scary a thought to contemplate: I was little while he was a big – very big by this point – wrestler. He wasn't keen on punches but, being a wrestler, he would grab my mother or me and shake, throttle and throw. I see my mother with sizeable bruises. In my memory, one morning she showed me the chopper she had slept with under her pillow because she was scared he might lose his temper in the middle of the night. It was a lethal combination.

My mother and stepfather married on the same day as my Uncle Eric's daughter. My mother made me brush my teeth and scrub my nails, and we had special outfits bought for us, not for her wedding but for my cousin's wedding. Uncle Eric was the wealthiest member of the family because he had invented the Decimetre, a pocket-sized currency calculator that converted the old money into new pence, so his daughter's wedding was a big do, Chelmsford Cathedral then on to the town hall function suite. I was eight, my sister was six and my brother was a babe in arms: he was violently sick all down my mother in the cathedral. I can remember my mum's outfit because I later tried it on. It was a brown-and-white floral miniskirt suit with a white floppy hat to match. My mother and stepfather had got married in the register office earlier that morning but I didn't know about it at the time and only found out later in the year – although it seemed to me that because my mother had got divorced once, divorce was always a possibility. My mother took my stepfather's name and my sister changed her surname for ease when she went to secondary school, but I didn't change my name, I didn't want to.

I once asked my mother, 'Did he hurt you last night?' to which she drawled, 'Ow, Yes!' in a suggestive, Kenneth Williams way. Early on they had love-ins, cuddled on the sofa and were robustly sexual. My mother was always open; she wouldn't mind me seeing her nude in the bath. She would say things like, 'Go and fetch me a sanitary towel,' whereas my stepfather disapproved of me walking about with only a towel round my waist when my sister was about. When my friends visited, my mother would get her tummy out, slap it on the kitchen table and brag, 'Look at that, you don't get many of them for the pound,' or, 'I've had a hysterectomy.' When she was showing one of my girlfriends around the house she would divulge, 'This is the room where Grayson does all his wanking.' My mother was staunchly working class, almost aggressively so, whereas my stepfather aspired to middle-class values. The day Mrs Thatcher came into power was the first time I voted and that morning I went with my mother in her rusty car that she delivered the papers in. We pulled up in front of the polling station in this clapped-out old Mini and the boot fell off with a clang. My mother shouted to the policeman, 'Here come the Labour voters. Yes, yes, we're Labour voters.' My mum voted Labour but my step-father was Conservative. She would never have voted what he voted. I am sure a lot of my rebelliousness, the style of it, comes from her.

My stepfather was a man of many fingers in many pies, big, stodgy, sausagy, scarred, knuckled fingers, jabby fingers on a jabbing hand, making assertive, thrusting gestures. He was always packing a wad. My mother boasted, 'He's never got less than a hundred quid on him.' As well as buying a large white van and doing house clearances, he worked as a nightclub bouncer and owned the café opposite Hoffman's ball-bearing factory in Chelmsford called Brian's Caff, which his parents ran. We used to visit the café occasionally, though I could hardly bring myself to eat there because I knew the conditions the food was cooked in. My mother worked there – we were all working for him. He liked everyone to work as hard as he did. I had another brother, Daniel, who had been born in 1971, and when my brothers were nine and four the old man would drive them on their paper rounds before they went to school in the morning and they would run out of the van to deliver the papers.

The old man worked such long hours he hardly ever drove the E-type Jag, so his friend Little Jim – who was very short – used to exercise the car. Little Jim would take the Jag out for a thrash, then park it on the drive underneath my bedroom window, its huge, shining bonnet up with the whopping great engine ticking, tick, tick, tick and steaming as it cooled down into the night. I used to have the top bunk bed, with Neil underneath, so I could look out of our bedroom window while I was lying in bed at night and watch the car steam. Little Jim would bring his son round with him and the son would sit there pulling his eyelashes out. I thought he was distinctly odd, though I don't think I qualified as normal.

When I've dreamed about my stepfather in my adult life he yodels a cry of frustration. In my childhood he would indeed let out a frustrated animal scream, usually because my mother had wound him up until he snapped – '*OOOWWWWWWWWWWWW!*' Then he would grab something or somebody, my mother or one of us. If he grabbed me he would slam me against the wall. One morning I came downstairs to find the sitting room in chaos where he had hurled furniture about and there were holes in the door where he had punched it. Another night he pulled the door shut so very hard he bent the door handle right round. He would throw the electric fire, chairs, even the sofa.

I was tense in his presence and his was a brooding presence, like a sleeping dragon you shouldn't disturb. He was a storm on the horizon, which broke all the time: if I didn't do the washing up or I didn't do the washing up properly, if I was sick in the car or if I annoyed my mother over something or other, he would be summoned. Mum was like the ground troops; he would be called in like an air strike on a bombing run. I was ordered up to my bedroom, then given the traditional whack on the arse because he administered spankings if there was a recognised crime, like a broken lampshade. There was an animalistic rivalry between us, but I was a scrawny, pale blond; I wasn't a powerhouse, I was an endurance athlete. My mother frequently commented with some pride, 'You *never* answer back,' to which I thought, 'Yes! Survival mechanism!' From my childhood I developed guerrilla tactics – there was no sense in confronting the enemy head on, it was futile retaliating against someone who was much

I am My Own God, 1998

64

stronger. Messages were coming from Grayson Perry Central announcing, 'I WILL SURVIVE! This is a war of skirmishes and I will score my points by being clever, by escaping as soon as I can, by not giving them any of my talents. My talents are mine. My achievements are mine. I will not allow them to share in my glory.' My only weapon now is my forgiveness. It's invariably awful being on the end of other people's forgiveness.

I lived in the same house as my stepfather for fifteen years although I never had a conversation with him, certainly nothing longer than an exchange of a few sentences, usually of a functional nature. The commonest was, 'Do the washing up or your mother will get upset.' Often he talked to me in the third person or via a third person: 'Tell that long streak of piss to get off the sofa,' or, 'Could that Herbert do something to help his mother?' He hardly ever called me by my name, Grayson, it was always 'you' or an insult, nor did I address him by his name; I somehow got his attention to say what I needed to say. It was incredibly hard work and extremely tense. It was as if we didn't exist to each other. I never thought of calling him 'Dad', 'Dad' would have stuck in my throat. Calling people by their name is the beginning of an intimacy: having conversations, being able to fight back, are important components in forming a relationship.

My stepfather made his best efforts to have a working relationship with me, I imagine. He bought me an air rifle that I prized for many years until I shot my brother, Neil, with it and had it confiscated. I used to build a lot of little dens with my brothers and we would sit in our den with my air rifle and shoot things. I shot a bird once and felt terribly guilty. I was very much a surrogate father to my youngest brother, Daniel, and I played a lot with him when he was small. He was more sensitive than Neil, who was sporty and played football. I was the one who would mend the punctures on their bikes and build go-karts and play soldiers.

At Christmas there was always an exchange of gifts and he gave me *The Times World Atlas*, which I treasured. Christmas Day was symptomatic in our house in that we all, rather sadly, opened our presents in our own bedrooms, which I thought was normal until I went to someone else's house at Christmas and was stunned that other people opened their presents together – that nakedness was shocking to me. All my presents would be in my room when I woke up and I'd open them, then later on there would be a cursory 'Thank you'. It was very isolating.

My first inkling that my stepfather had sadness in his childhood was when his parents came to visit. His mother looked like the portrait in the National Gallery of the woman with the turned-up nose and the horrible, squidgy breasts pushed up in a bodice. They brought some of my stepfather's old toys from his boyhood but none of them had been played with. There was a clockwork man in its box that was over twenty years old yet still pristine and an untouched colouring book called *Sketches of the Stars* with a blank page opposite each picture where you could copy your sketch of the Hollywood film star from the early fifties. I don't think my stepfather had what I had in spades, which was a rich interior life.

Between the ages of four to fifteen, I gradually retreated further inwards and my internal world became increasingly important to me. I spent most of my time in my bedroom embellishing Alan Measles's domain. I would go upstairs and free fall almost, riff on what I was feeling, then play out those feelings in my game – so there would be a lot of war! With the Germans. I played out these events in detailed scenarios involving cars, tanks and my ever-growing collection of model aeroplanes. Events were upsetting, terrifying, much of the time and if I had allowed emotion to flood in it would have been overwhelming, so I dealt with the highs and lows by being numb. Any feeling of love I had was shut down. I must have loved my mother. Parents are a child's survival. When I was a child, how could I countenance not thinking my parents were perfect? The alternative was too frightening to think of.

9

STUPIDER THAN ME

I was a child who knew I was cuckoo in the nest, who knew that my parents were *stupider* than me. Even though I didn't acknowledge it consciously, I realised it subconsciously. My parents patronised me because they couldn't understand me. It was, 'Oh, isn't he clever!' It was as if I were a zoo monster wheeled out for guests: 'Look at the models Grayson's made this week,' or, 'Have you seen his drawings!' Visitors would be shown my room as if I were a weird Outsider Artist: 'Here's Grayson's room' and the subtext would be, 'Isn't it odd to have this kid in the house!'

There weren't any books at home, even though by then we were newsagents too. My stepfather struggled to fill in the children's crossword in the *Sun*. I had a few books because I read voraciously, beginning with Dr Doolittle, then James Bond and all the *Boy's Own* adventures. My sister dipped into *My Friend Flicka* and my mother would leaf through *Woman*, *Woman's Own*, the *Sun* and the *Mirror*. My mother realised the value of education, though: she was the one who entered me for grammar school. She recognised I was intelligent. My mother often remarked, 'He's done it all on his own.'

My school was a venerable grammar school for boys, founded in 1555 by King Edward the Sixth. Academically it was the best school in Essex, to get in you had to be in the top five per cent in the country in the 11-plus. It had an excellent reputation and a very good relationship with Oxbridge. Unencumbered, maybe I would have studied at Oxford or Cambridge and had a different life, becoming an academic and finding fulfilment in an alternative way. Curiously, the school backed on to a school for the mentally handicapped, which I always thought was ironic. It had been a boarding school and still had the atmosphere of a traditional public school: there were quadrangles, quirky jargon and the teachers wore gowns. It was a culture shock. A well-spoken woman in the village said to my mother, 'My son is going to King Edward the Sixth Grammar School in September, it's an excellent school and in the top five state schools in the country,' to which my mother rejoined, 'Ow! That's where my Grayson's going!' and enjoyed watching the woman deflate.

The uniform was black, with a blazer that had red braid round the collar for the first three years. It was de rigueur to get this as dirty as possible as soon as possible because glowing red braid round your lapel was a sign of naffness. I had a satchel but there was no chance I was going to be bought a new bag until it wore out, so for the first four years I had this satchel, which was a badge of geekiness. Everybody else had an Adidas sports bag: that was a source

69

of agony and angst for me. As I always lived a long way from school I didn't have a social life connected with school; I was a bit of a loner-weirdo on the periphery.

In the first year I was in the middle of my class, in the second year I was top of the class, winning the form prize. For my prize I chose a book called *How to Go: Plastic Modelling*. In the third year I was sixth from bottom and the school were curious; they wanted to know what had happened. What had happened was that one day the old man had picked me up, banged me against the wall, then almost thrown me up the stairs. I phoned my grandmother in panic, blurting, 'He's gone mad! I'm terrified!' My grandmother immediately called the NSPCC. The school must have been informed by the charity and, with my results plummeting, have put two and two together.

The RE teacher walked into the middle of a lesson barking, 'I want to talk to you.' He was stern. Despite being the vicar, he was also one of the major disciplinarians in school so he gave off mixed messages. He took me into his little office – he was the nearest we had to a school counsellor but he wasn't very good. He asked me a few questions about my home life, so I stated the bald facts and felt a bit teary. He asked, 'Did he . . . ?' and I replied, 'Yeah . . . blah blah blah. Violent, blah blah blah.' All of a sudden, the NSPCC were at the house. It was a mystery to me at the time why they arrived, nor did I have any idea of the seriousness of it. The woman, who was a mousy lady with round glasses, took me upstairs to my bedroom to speak to me on my own in private. She asked about the situation and how I felt. I was so out of touch with myself that she was talking to a cipher and

I can't imagine she got any information out of me, certainly not enough for them to be able to take action. Then we all sat down on the sofa as a family in the sitting room while the mousy lady asked me 'Do you love your stepfather?' and I parroted 'Yes', because I was sitting in front of the man who held the sword of Damocles hanging over me so I wasn't going to reply, 'No! He's a fucking bastard! He's a fucking bastard!' This woman was going to leave but I was going to have to go on living with the old man, so I wasn't going to say, 'I fucking hate his guts.' The mousy woman left and nothing else happened after that; I didn't hear hide or hair of it again.

I retreated more and more into the haven of my bedroom. There wasn't a scrap of wallpaper showing in there because it was covered with pictures of aeroplanes, every sort of aeroplane. My favourites were the American 1950s and 1960s jet fighters because they were flashier than the RAF version. The British ones were always dark green; the American ones were cartoon-like, painted silver with a tiger's mouth on the front, or a heraldic device on the side. I had dozens of model aeroplanes, made from Airfix kits. Uncle Arthur built me a special shelf for my models, but that very quickly became colonised. The pelmet, the windowsill, the table, everywhere was spread with models. By the time I was fifteen I had over a hundred. I bought all the model-making magazines and studied them, then made the models better than the kit instructions. I was avid about model building in a very detailed way. The kit was only the starting point: I would add parts to get the fine detail. It was about minutiae, realism and doing things to make the aeroplanes look worn, which was called weathering. *Really* painstaking. Putting in exhaust fume marks where the exhaust had stained the paint and making little scratches where the pilots had climbed into the cockpit. I would sand the bottom of the wheels to make them oval because the tyres would squash with the weight of the aeroplane.

Model Jet Plane X92, 1999

The guns and tanks I made models of I was having first-hand experience of in the Cadet Force. Between the ages of fourteen and sixteen the Cadet Force got me out of the house, gave me contact with guns and tanks and offered me *Boy's Own* fun. I relished all the drills, the shooting, the charging around in the forest and crawling about in the undergrowth with guns pretending to fight each other. Going to camp was fantastic fun; we paid £2 for a fortnight in an army camp in Wales where we would set off on marches, race through assault courses and climb mountains. The other cadets pulled my sleeping bag off me one morning and chanted, 'Perry, the pubeless wonder!' I thoroughly enjoyed the Army Cadet life with its camaraderie. I was very disciplined, hard-working and physical, I was the fastest in the whole cadet force around the assault course, always looked very smart and I quickly got promoted so I decided, 'I'm going to join the army.' I was going to be an officer. I would do my A levels and then go to Sandhurst. I wanted that. I don't think it would have suited me, I think I would have killed myself or somebody else – a lot of other people probably, mainly dark men, I imagine, who were milkmen. I would have picked off any milkmen at five hundred yards with a laser gun. Boom! That was my plan and my mother thought it was a very good one. If I was emotionally stunted, I didn't need to be anything else for the army: I was ideal fodder!

In the autumn of 1975, when I was fifteen and just after I had decided to become an officer, I stumbled across an article in the *News of the World* about transvestites and sex changes, with a photograph of April Ashley, a model and socialite, one of the first well-known transsexuals who had scandalously married an aristocrat. I knew now that transvestism was a phenomenon that existed. I developed the typical transvestite fantasies of waking up in the morning to discover I had become a girl. I would look longingly at schoolgirls, thinking, 'Oh God, I *wish* I could dress like that.' Newsreaders were my fantasy goal. If only I could wake up in the morning and be Anna Ford, or Sue Lawley from *Nationwide* with her neat hair and her trendy dresses. I began experimenting with my mum's make-up. I paraded around the house dressed up and gazed at myself in the mirror with the make-up on. I now knew this was a transvestite occupation. I was padding out a bra with socks and borrowing a pair of tights and shoes – I could just about squeeze into my mother's shoes. All I needed was a wig. I wanted a wig because I had a skinhead haircut. The rebellious group of lads I'd fallen in with, all of whom had skinheads, had persuaded me to go to the barber with them to have a Number 2 – my mother was horrified and, because I was thin, she called me Belsen Annie.

In the back pages of the *Daily Mail* there were adverts for cut-price wigs. For some reason, God knows what, I fancied being auburn so I ordered an auburn wig in a bob hairstyle. I paid £1 – I couldn't believe a wig was so cheap. It must have been awful for a quid. I thought, 'How am I going to send off for one? I can't have one delivered to the house.' I told my best friend, Tom Edwards, that I was buying a Christmas present for my mum but wanted it to be a surprise. I addressed the wig to the Edwardses' house and one week later Tom gave me a parcel at the bus stop. Finally, I had a complete outfit.

As soon as I learned the word transvestite, I researched it in the psychology books in Chelmsford library. There was a noted textbook called *Sexual Deviations* that

74

included a couple of case studies. I looked up 'transvestite' and read. I learned that going out dressed up was one of the things cross-dressers did. On 5 November 1975, which I now call Claire's birthday, I put on the full rig and stepped out of the front door. There I stood in my lipstick, blue chiffon headscarf over my auburn wig, a brown polyester blouse and black-and-white dog-tooth check skirt, tan tights, black court shoes and a beige mac: a middle-aged look. 'She' was I, Grayson, she had no name, she wasn't yet Claire. It was thrilling. It was icily cold and the cold still has an erotic charge for me because of that day. My sex drive takes a leap when the temperature drops; it is conditioned by those early experiences. For some silly reason Transvestite Day is 4 August whereas it should be something like 27 January. Winter is the trannie season because it's chilly, you're wearing a wig and lots of padding, which is hot; it's also dark so you can sneak out of the house without the neighbours seeing, and you can cover up with a coat.

At nine o'clock in the morning, taking enormous risks, I walked down our lane, round the village, then back home and I was on cloud nine, having the time of my life. It was the most exhilarating thing I had ever done. As I couldn't see myself in the mirror while I was walking through the village, the cliché of the nippy air round my legs along with the physical feeling of wearing uncomfortable shoes constantly reminded me that I was wearing cramped, female clothes. The perfect transvestite experience would be traipsing along the street with someone holding a gigantic mirror in front of me so that I could see myself the whole time and know exactly what I looked like. As I can't watch myself, wearing crippling shoes, being a tad cold or having unusual physical sensations from my outfit remind me that I'm in the wrong clothes. It accentuates the difference.

Even though I had learned I was a transvestite, I was realising I was wholly heterosexual and was fantasising about girls but, because I went to an all-boys school, girls were foreign territory and petrifying. At primary school a girl had pinned me down in the playground and kissed me, and I remember thinking later on, 'Oh God! I didn't take enough advantage of that situation.' When my sister had her tenth birthday party all her friends arrived wearing their party togs; this was the early seventies and a little-girl look was fashionable. One of the guests wore a blue-and-yellow, little-girl-style Crimplene dress with pretty cherries on it. I saw that dress and fell utterly in love with it. When we played Murder in the Dark I had a surreptitious feel of her frock, I couldn't help myself whispering, 'Ohhhhhhh!' It was electrifying and I desperately wanted that dress. She looked sweet in it and I wanted to be her.

IO

I WAS DOROTHY, SHE WAS THE WHIRLWIND

A school friend asked me, 'Is your dad Derek Perry? When I said he was he went on, 'I'm going out with his adopted daughter.'

I thought, 'That's interesting.' I didn't know anything about my father, not even where he was living; I hadn't seen him since I was seven and now I was fifteen. My father wasn't someone I knew any more, he was a mythic, hazy figure who wasn't my stepfather and who hopefully offered to fill the hero's role, the Alan Measles role. In my teenage brain I thought, 'My father might offer me a way out of my situation. He might rescue me.'

I arranged to meet my father's adopted daughter and one lunchtime I went with her to my father's house. There I met his second wife, Maureen-Ann, and I told her, 'I'd like to meet my father again.' Maureen-Ann was friendly, perhaps she was surprised by my visit, I don't know, because I saw the unfolding of events from my point of view, not thinking of the import and impact my appearance would have. I was in an intolerable situation, my home life and my sexuality were pressing in on me, I was taking wild measures, so going to see Maureen-Ann seemed inconsequential.

The following Saturday I told my mother, 'I've got a hockey match today,' but instead of playing hockey, I went to meet my father. I couldn't tell my mother where I was going because my father's name was mud in her house. I arrived at his home in Chelmsford, this skinny, shaven-headed teenager in Doc Martens and a combat jacket, a tuff-stuff carapace but all wet inside, for my first meeting with him in eight years. He was in bed. I walked into his bedroom, mumbling, 'Oh, hello.' He wasn't King of All the Universe, Alan Measles. There was a huge gulf between the attention I wanted from him and the attention he could give me. We spent the day together tinkering around with his old Bedford van – a very Derek Perry scenario: he was always tinkering around with cars. On the way home I dirtied my hockey kit on a piece of muddy ground so that it looked as if I'd worn it.

Meanwhile, that autumn my stepfather had decided to build a house in a village called Great Bardfield so he bought a fourteen-acre field that used to be a chicken farm and got planning permission to build a big house in this field. By early December our house was sold, we were already beginning to pack and soon we were all going to move into two caravans in the field while the house was built. My stepfather also wanted to buy the local newsagent's business in which the whole family would have to be involved. The deadline was looming. It was a horrific thought, moving just before Christmas into a small caravan in a wet field next to a building site, two hours from my school and my friends. My needs were down at the bottom of a long, long list of other considerations. Part of me was shouting, 'Get out of here. No one gives a shit about what you feel.'

I arranged to stay the weekend with my father because I was observing his house, thinking, 'Here's a lifeboat, I'm going to leap into it.' I took my army bag with my uniform, pretending to my mother that I was going away with the Cadet Force – I was getting quite deceitful. That weekend my father took me for an Indian, which was the first time I had eaten in a proper restaurant, and he got me drunk on Irish coffees. I had a nice time. My father's house seemed a more liberal and relaxed household. I don't know what he thought, I don't think he realised how oppressive it felt at home because I wouldn't have been at all communicative about how violent I felt my stepfather was and how frightened I was.

One evening in early December when we were on the very brink of moving into the caravans, I casually mentioned to my mother that I'd seen my father recently. She started shouting and screaming, and was incredibly angry. There was a lot of 'After all these years . . . blah, blah, blah and you want to . . . blah, blah, blah'. So I was sucked into her vortex of drama: I was Dorothy, she was the whirlwind. As soon as I mentioned that I'd seen my father she shrieked, 'And I suppose *you* want to go and live with *him*?'

She suggested it and I floundered, 'Well, yeah. I would.'

She made the decision for me. She exclaimed, 'Right then! We'll pack!' She demanded my father's telephone number and although she'd had no contact with him or

Maureen-Ann, she rang their house – my father wasn't even there – announcing, 'Right! I'm bringing Grayson over. He's coming to live with you.' Within half an hour she was driving me to my father's. We rustled together my clothes, of which there weren't many, she drove me into Chelmsford and left me at the top of the street where my father lived – she didn't even drive me up to the house – and then drove away. It was a very cold, frosty night.

There I was, dumped and shell-shocked – I'd only seen my father twice in eight years, both times at my suggestion. I walked down the road carrying my holdall and there I was, completely numb, at my father's front door. I arrived in this other household in rather a hurry. I was put into the lodger's room; I can't imagine the lodger was very happy having the son plonked in his room. My father came back the next day and dealt with it, God knows how. We got by. There were a few tearful phone calls from my mother, but she didn't ask me to come back.

My father lived in a very cramped, overcrowded end-of-terrace council house in Chelmsford. He had taken it upon himself to rescue and adopt Maureen-Ann's children, whom she had let go of and who were almost the same age as my sister and I. He found the daughter, Belinda, dirty and unkempt, in a squalid flat in Sheffield in atrocious conditions: 'Like the third world,' he claimed. Next he collected the son, Pete, from a children's home. My father had then set up home with Maureen-Ann and his adopted children. My grandfather, a gentle soul, was living with him as well because his wife had an affair and divorced him when they were both pensioners. My grandfather had one room, which he shared with his blaring black-and-white telly, Belinda had another, Maureen-Ann and my father had the largest bedroom and the lodger and I shared the box room. The box room was previously the son's room – Pete was a hippy who had moved to Brighton. He was legendary because he was caught growing cannabis on the railway embankment behind the terrace causing the police to raid the house. Pete's old room was a hippy's fantasy drug room. It had carpet on one wall and silver foil on the other. There were peacock feathers, Hendrix posters and sculptures made from wig heads, but as it was 1975 and the birth of punk, this hippy room with its black ceiling decorated with fluorescent stars seemed almost old-fashioned and nostalgic. It was very oppressive.

Charlie, the lodger, was Pete's friend. He worked on a burger van at night and slept in the day, which meant that we weren't on top of each other because when he was out I was in. There were also Maureen-Ann's two skinny, yappy, shivery Chihuahuas with their bulging eyes skipping around the house. I always hated Chihuahuas.

As soon as I moved into the box room I became utterly obsessed, in my teenage mind, with getting hold of some women's clothes. The transvestite urge was powerful. It was fresh, novel, exciting but it had been nipped in the bud by the move, the resulting upheaval and my limited access to privacy. Being in this busy little council house that was never empty, that always had someone in it, I was never going to be able to dress up there. How was I going to dress? I started hatching plans.

I began scoping public spaces all over Chelmsford for discreet toilets. I was assessing them for privacy, infrequency of use, lighting and whether there was a mirror. The best toilets I found were behind Chelmsford museum. They were 1930s public conveniences, underused and covered with bushes. I packed all my women's stuff into my Adidas bag, including the stash of women's clothes that I'd borrowed from my mother. I had the rudiments; I had shoes, and some old make-up I had found in my mother's chest of drawers and my auburn wig. I went through Maureen-Ann's wardrobe: unfortunately she was a small woman and I was already quite a large boy. I borrowed one of her dresses that would have been entirely inappropriate and out of fashion by then: she clung on to the miniskirt longer than most people did, so her dresses were extremely short. There was a tweed cape and I borrowed that too. I shoved all this stuff into my Adidas bag, then cycled to Central Park in Chelmsford after school, sneaked into the women's lavatory, dressed up and tottered round the park. I hid my bag in the bushes, which in itself was a dangerous thing to do, because if it had been stolen while I was walking about . . . I was freezing and probably looked like a prostitute in the miniskirt. I had a bad auburn wig on and cheap make-up applied in a freezing cold toilet, but I was soft of feature and very slender, and I would have looked quite feminine. I wandered around Central Park for a little while, then got changed back, and I realised I'd got away with it and it had worked.

I kept on dressing up and it became an overriding obsession. I developed a strategy that ensured I always came out of the appropriate toilet. Emerge from the men's toilet dressed as a man and from the women's toilet as a woman – that's how I did it tactically. I dressed up half a dozen times over the next month or two. It was always perishingly cold. Although it was the middle of winter in a stinky little public toilet in a park, the cold was exciting as I was constantly aware of not wearing enough clothes and having exposed legs in my tights.

I became bolder and started wandering down into Chelmsford. I bought some make-up at a chemist's and I wasn't hassled. I don't think people could work me out: I probably looked like an odd young woman in a wig, or a mad, slightly druggy prostitute. I would have been a tall, gangly woman in too short an outfit for a chilly midwinter day and not fashionable in the slightest. Luckily, I had blond hair on my legs so I didn't have to walk about looking like a gorilla. The skirts by early 1976 had got longer but I was wearing Maureen-Ann's older clothes, not those she was using at the time because that seemed too risky. I was wearing clothing from the back of her wardrobe that I never saw her in, cute minidresses and the mini cape, which was also very short.

My first inkling of how I looked came when I was walking down Moulsham Street in Chelmsford and a bloke in a Jag shouted at me, 'Helloooooooo darling!' as if he knew me.

I thought, 'He thinks I'm a prostitute.'

This man stopped his car asking, 'Hello! Do I know you?' then began questioning me: 'What's your name? Where do you live?'

I answered him in a soft voice but inside I was frightened. Perhaps he was another trannie, maybe he thought I was a girl prostitute or a boy prostitute or possibly he really did think I was a woman walking around in a bad wig and a miniskirt. I fantasised afterwards: 'What would have happened if I'd got in his car?' It would have been an extremely dangerous thing to do.

I had to get changed back into my normal clothes in the privacy of a toilet cubicle. I was washing off my make-up with the water from the toilet bowl. It was difficult to remove the mascara. I had blond eyelashes so it would be noticeable if I was darker around the eye. Every time I returned to the house, I had to sneak Maureen-Ann's clothes back into her wardrobe, which was another risk. Nevertheless, dressing up was an exciting project. It involved the skulking around of the Cadet Force combined with an incredible sexual thrill. I was mainlining on adrenalin. It was like injecting adrenalin as if it were heroin.

Before long, I found an overgrown toilet in Chelmsford's municipal cemetery. An old laurel bush had grown over the entrance so that it was hidden, and the Men's and Women's were next to each other. It looked like it was hardly ever used so I could take my time. It was ideal for my purposes. I used to spend my Saturday afternoons putting on make-up in the cemetery toilets, then traipsing around the gravestones.

One Saturday I was wandering around the graveyard in my women's clothes when I found a lady's bicycle, so I took it. I stole this bicycle, riding a couple of miles down the lane to another toilet, by which time I was cold, I wanted to change back and I was worried about having a stolen bike. These other toilets were exposed, badly vandalised and the Ladies' and Gent's signs had been chiselled off. I walked through one entrance hoping it was the Gent's, realising, 'Oh fuck, it's the Women's,' which

Tomb Model, 1998

meant I would have to emerge from the Ladies as a man. No one was around so I thought, 'I'm not going to go out and go round to the Men's, I'll just get changed in here.'

When I came out a couple of park wardens were sitting in a car nearby. I got on my stolen bike and as I cycled past they shouted, 'Hey! Mate! Come over here!' They stated, 'You've just come out of the Ladies.'

I replied, 'Yeah, I know, the signs are missing.'

They said, 'All right, but don't do it again,' so I got away with it but it scared me because I could have been caught for dressing up. The repercussions of being taken home dressed as a woman in Maureen-Ann's clothes would have been difficult. It would have hurried along the inevitable. That was the last time I dressed up before the shit hit the fan.

A few weeks later I mentioned to my dad, 'I'm going to play with the hockey team on Saturday afternoon.'

He replied, 'Oh, I'll think about that.'

I queried, 'What do you mean?'

He said, 'I don't know if I'm going to let you.' Then he announced, 'I want to have a little chat with you.' He took me upstairs, sat me down on my bed and proclaimed, 'I've found out about your little game.' At first I thought he meant some kind of petty criminal activity I'd been up to with my friends. He added, 'You're dressing up.'

I went completely numb and depressed. I asked, 'How did you find out?'

He muttered 'Oh, we've got ways.'

What had happened was that Belinda had found my diary, which had a few notes in it about my cross-dressing adventures. I was fervently researching transvestism in Chelmsford Central Library where I was intently reading through all the textbooks on psychology and sexual deviation. I spent a lot of time in the library getting a hard-on reading case studies. The word 'transvestite' was written on a page in my diary. Belinda had read my journal then asked her mother, 'What does "transvestite" mean?'

Maureen-Ann wanted to know, 'Where did you read that?'

To which Belinda replied, 'In Grayson's diary.'

Maureen-Ann was incensed that I had used her clothes and I'd been doing what she imagined young transvestites do in women's clothes, and she was probably right: wanking! She telephoned my mother, my stepfather and my Aunty Mary and Uncle Arthur, telling them all that I had been dressing up in her clothes. She spread the news so that everybody knew. My mother came to visit me demand-

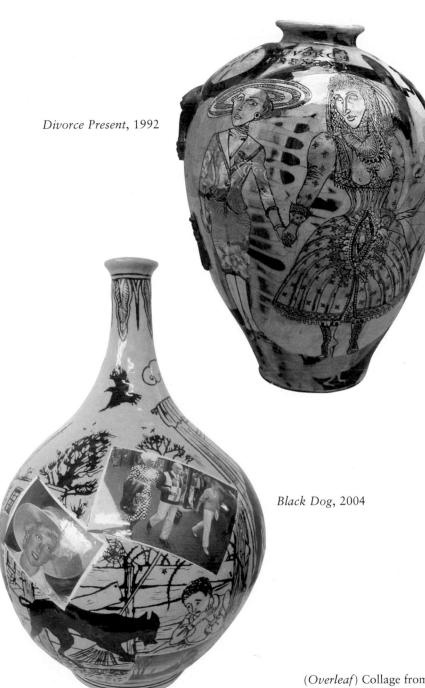

Divorce Present, 1992

Black Dog, 2004

(*Overleaf*) Collage from
an early sketchbook

'One must suffer like a woman'

Neo-naturist,
as Burnham Wood

Grayson in the squat
as Claire

(*Overleaf*) Grayson and
Claire by the stream,
moon spinning dreams

THE QUEEN OF THE SKY BUSILY TURNING CLOUDS

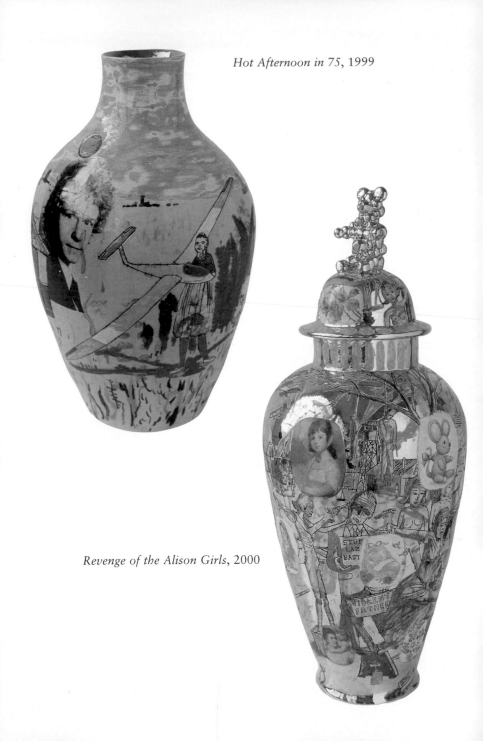

Hot Afternoon in 75, 1999

Revenge of the Alison Girls, 2000

ing to know, 'What's this about you dressing up?' I remember her exclaiming, 'You went out of *our* house dressed in *my* clothes!'

My stepfather proclaimed, 'That's it! You're never seeing your brothers again.' He thought that I was some sort of pervert. In a way, I was some sort of pervert, but not the sort of pervert that he thought. I was frightened, sad and depressed, and I was in shock all the time.

Charlie, the lodger, a happy-go-lucky, chirpy chap who was very tolerant in putting up with all that was going on, sensed something was happening. He came downstairs jesting, 'What's going on then? What's going on then? Grayson in trouble, is he?'

My dad muttered, 'Yeah, he is a bit.'

So Charlie piped up, 'What's he done then, got a girl pregnant, has he?'

My father and Maureen-Ann searched the box room, discovered my suitcase with women's clothes under the bed and confiscated them. They sent me to the GP, who examined me physically. The GP thought dressing up was to do with being gay, asking me if anyone else was involved. I retorted, 'No! I just dress up on my own.' My dad booked me an appointment with the psychiatrist in Chelmsford hospital but I told him, 'I'm not going. I'm all right. I'm over it.' And that was it, I got away with it. They believed me, God Almighty! They were all so uncomfortable with it that if it could be swept under the carpet they were happy.

It was while my transvestism was being revealed that I got into trouble with the police. I thought, 'This will show them that I'm a *real* man.' I was friendly with three local lads and there was talk of us nicking mopeds. One of them said, 'I saw this moped at the station – it was unlocked.' So we sauntered round to Chelmsford train station where one of the lads got on the moped, started it up then rode off, but we were quickly forced to dump it because it ran out of petrol. We'd loped off to the park, gone, 'Ha, ha, ha,' then decided, 'We could go back, get the moped and ride it round the fields.' I was dispatched to cycle past where we had left the bike to check the coast was clear, not thinking I was wearing my very distinctive Army Cadet jumper. However, we'd been seen earlier and now there was a detective waiting. He started to chase me down the road in his police car. He pulled up next to me with a whheeerrrrrre, forcing me to halt, charged out into the road and grabbed hold of me. That was me banged up. I was taken into Chelmsford police station, put into a cell and questioned. I cracked! I spilt the beans – I was petrified – I told them who everybody was although I felt bad letting my friends down. We got off with a caution. My friends forgave me, which was a relief as I was scared that they would hate me for it.

The detective took me back to my dad's house in a police car because he needed my father's permission to fingerprint me and I was so frightened of what my father's reaction would be that I thought, 'Oh God! Maybe I can do a runner when the police car stops.' I was surprised by how relaxed my father's response was; I put it down to him being so relieved I'd done something boyish. That evening he confided to me that he'd once been in trouble with the law himself.

In time my life settled down to a certain extent. I took

my O levels and was lining up to do my A levels and to go to Sandhurst. I spent many hours in my father's shed building an elaborate motorboat that never saw the water, I cycled over to visit Aunty Mary and Uncle Arthur and I started doing a paper round in Chelmsford hospital. I got up early every morning; walked to the newsagent's nearest the hospital, collected a bag of papers and sold them to the patients. I enjoyed going round the wards with the little old ladies asking me, 'Can I have a *People's Friend* tomorrow?' so I'd bring them one the next morning. They were very trusting and loving, letting me rummage in their handbags to get the change. There were the private wards, which was where I sold the *Daily Express*, the *Daily Mail* and the *Daily Telegraph* – everybody else bought the *Sun* or the *Mirror*. Sometimes I would see spooky things: people dying, the curtains being drawn around them and the family looking grief-stricken. I caught a man wanking once. I used to poke my head through the curtains, probably not the thing to do, and there he was giving it beans.

I got up on my sixteenth birthday but my father hadn't remembered – nobody had remembered – it was my birthday. When I arrived at school one of my friends asked me, 'How are you today, Grayson?'

I said, 'It's my birthday,' and he wished me happy birthday. I mumbled, 'You're the first person to say that to me today.' When I got home, my father had remembered after all; he was a bit sheepish and he gave me three pounds. My mum had forgotten too.

In the summer of 1976 we went on holiday to a vast caravan park in West Bay, Dorset. My dad, Maureen-Ann,

Belinda and I went with Pippa, her husband and their two kids. Pippa was the next-door neighbour and we had caravans next to each other. Her husband had a car with blue-tinted windows and he spent the entire time scraping off the tinting with a razor blade. During the holiday my father and Maureen-Ann had a vicious row, but to me a vicious row was normal. She protested that my father had hit her and put on make-up to make her look like she was bruised. When they had a screaming, violent argument, I thought, 'Oh well, back to normal.'

There I was, a testosterone-fuelled boy in a cap-sleeved T-shirt and baggies on a caravan site. Three caravans away there was a girl called Sally who took an interest in me and we began holding hands and quickly paired up. We went for long walks over the clifftops – God knows what drivel I talked as my conversation consisted entirely of me telling endless numbers of very weak jokes by rote – followed by a wet kiss at Sally's caravan door before we parted. So I got my first girlfriend. And on the last night I got my first sticky finger down her knickers: I managed to cop a feel, as they said in seventies parlance. It was innocent, wet bumbling-fumbling and I enjoyed it. I had broken my duck: I could attract women, I could kiss them and it was OK. Like getting in trouble with the police, it was a boyish vice and it had made me feel more secure.

I was spending every day with Sally and this annoyed Maureen-Ann mightily: Maureen-Ann wanted me to be gay because that would have fitted in with her worldview. The day before Sally and I paired off, Maureen-Ann had made a remark about me being queer but my dad scoffed, 'Don't be ridiculous! Haven't you seen the way the girls look at him?' As a man, he had picked up on the vibes and he knew I was getting female attention, so I was obviously giving off the right signals. My dad's instincts were right: I've never thought I was gay.

On the final day of the holiday it was Maureen-Ann's fortieth birthday so I thought, 'I'll buy Maureen-Ann a birthday card,' an innocent, well-meaning gesture. I chose a card with a little scraperboard picture of a black pig on it, which I thought was cute. Unbeknownst to me, Maureen-Ann had had a conversation with Pippa the previous evening saying, 'I always think people show exactly what they think of me with their birthday card.' Little did I know what she had been brewing while we were on holiday.

The moment we returned home Maureen-Ann exploded, attacking me for all the crimes I'd done against her, some of which were probably true. 'You fucking pervert! I don't want you near my daughter! You hate me; you gave me a birthday card with a black pig on it! Get out of my house now. Don't *ever* come back.'

I got on my bike and pedalled furiously around Chelmsford trying to find refuge. First I headed for some close friends of my dad's who'd helped me with my Airfix models, but they were out. I cycled over to Aunty Mary's but she wasn't in either. I cycled round all day, getting very hungry, eventually ending up with the sympathetic neighbour opposite my father's house, who had picked up all my belongings, including my suitcase of women's clothes, when Maureen-Ann had thrown them out on to the doorstep. The neighbour knew about my dressing up because Maureen-Ann had assiduously told everyone. On my first day there my father came over with my O level results and I had passed nine. He didn't say to come back; perhaps because he wanted an easy life. This was now the second time he'd seen me drift away.

The next day my mother turned up. She said she had talked to the old man. She said, 'The old man's willing to take you back.'

MOONBOW

My mother drove me back that August afternoon to the caravans in the field on the outskirts of Great Bardfield, a pretty village in north Essex. My mother and stepfather were living in the caravan with the kitchen and we were in the other one. It was snug in our caravan because it had a coal fire and it was good to be back with my sister and brothers. My sister slept at one end and my brothers and I slept in three beds in a row, so it was very cosy and warm but with four children, aged sixteen, fourteen, nine and five, and an open fire it was a death trap. Whether we were aware of it or not, we were all under the tyranny of my stepfather, certainly we knew we had to tread carefully around the sleeping dragon.

On that first morning back I had the longest conversation I ever had with my stepfather – he was not an articulate man and I was so tense in his company. He took me on my own in his van to do the paper round because he wanted to talk to me about my dressing up. 'We don't want any more of that cross-dressing thing,' he grunted.

I squeaked, 'Oh no! Oh no! I've given that up, ha ha ha!' and maybe I thought I had, that I could. I had scant knowledge of what transvestism was.

My stepfather immediately allocated me a paper round. My round was the entire village and, as there was no longer a newsagent there, everyone had to have their papers delivered. On Friday night and Saturday morning I trudged round the village collecting the paper money, so I learned where everyone lived, what work they did, how many children they had and what they read – which was telling in itself. Most villagers had a tabloid or the *Telegraph*: it was a resolutely Conservative area with a few *Guardian* readers sprinkled in. My sister's boyfriend's father lived opposite the town hall and on polling day he decorated his whole house with Labour posters as a calculated affront to the local people. Ernie Hockley had huge hollyhocks growing in his garden and I used to say, 'There's Ernie Hockley's hollyhocks.' Two hippies bought the Lamb, the beautiful but derelict pub: I had to weave around rusting Morris Minors in the pub courtyard to push the *Observer* through a slot in the brickwork. In the middle of the village there was the doctor's surgery. Both the doctors committed suicide, first the husband, then the wife. There were also quirky, possibly inbred, slightly bonkers country folk who lived a very rural existence. A lovely old cowman with no roof to his mouth bicycled through Bardfield every morning on his way to milk the cows, a very friendly character who always had a daily paper. I got to know all the housewives and had fantasies about the prettier ones inviting me in for sex. There were a couple of opportunities but I was too young to take advantage of them.

Within a few months I could say hello to everyone in the village and at Christmas I received a lot of tips, the equivalent of a week's wages. I was known as the newsagent's son. My name, then, was Grayson Cousins. My sister had changed her name and my mother was eager for me to adopt my stepfather's surname because she didn't want anyone to know that this was her second marriage. She told everyone I was in the army, which was why I hadn't been there for nine months and then suddenly appeared, though I made no effort to keep up her charade. I wasn't Grayson Cousins at school or with my friends. My stepfather paid me thirty-five pence an hour, which was eight pounds for a twenty-four-hour week. Perhaps he reasoned he paid for my keep, and I was willing to trade on that. I wasn't in a bargaining position. If the newspapers were printed they had to be distributed so I

With my sister and brothers, 1974

95

worked seven days a week, three hundred and sixty-two days a year, getting up at half past five to deliver papers for two hours, but I survived it. I did it. I was very thin, very fit, I was an energetic boy and I was motivated because I was frightened. I learned the round easily, I remembered how much people owed, I could calculate the money in my head, I could handle the cash and I was honest.

I never did my homework nor did I visit Aunty Mary and Uncle Arthur, because I didn't have the energy. I always fell asleep on the two-hour bus journey to and from school. I fell asleep at school in lessons but never in art lessons – I loved art lessons and did extra art in the lunchtimes. I did an intricate pen drawing of a giant woman in Victorian dress towering over a row of houses, which Mr Shash, the art teacher, liked. He said, 'I'll put that up on parents' night, Grayson.' Afterwards he remarked, 'A lot of parents made comments about your drawing.'

When Mr Shash asked me in my Lower Sixth year, 'Have you thought of going to art college? I think you'd really like it. You'd do very well,' a switch was thrown, clunk! And a light bulb popped.

I replied, 'Sounds like a good idea. How do you go about that then?' I had no conception that there was a formal, academic training to become an artist. In that moment I made my decision, wrote it on a piece of paper in my mind, put it under a mental mattress, slept on it and never needed to look at it again: 'I'm going to be an artist. I'm going to spend my life drawing for a living.' It seemed like a fantastic idea because I loved drawing. I went home that day and announced, 'I'm going to go to art college.' I think my mum was disappointed because art wasn't thought of as a proper career and until that moment I was still intending to go to Sandhurst.

The academic requirement to get into college was five O levels, which I already had, so I let my Geography and English A levels slide, although I worked hard for Art A level. I scraped through Geography and failed English. In English A level we studied stolid classics: Shakespeare, Chaucer and Jane Austen, very hard work for a testosterone-loaded seventeen-year-old. We read *Emma* but I was the wrong sex and an emotional illiterate. It seemed to me the most boring, trivial of books with no action at all. We studied *David Copperfield* and I enjoyed that, but not *Emma*. When we did *King Lear* I can remember thinking, 'There's a bit of something going on here.'

The building on the new house was soon finished and we moved out of the caravans and into Pant Ken. The house was called Pant Ken because the River Pant flowed along the bottom of the field and Ken was my stepfather's middle name. It was substantial, five-bedroomed and hideously ugly, without any architectural merit, like a clumpy Barrett home. The lounge had an elongated York-stone fireplace, ranch-style, surrounded by beige shag-pile carpet so long you could lose a cat in it. The carpet needed raking rather than hoovering.

The old man had a routine in Pant Ken. He drove to Braintree to collect the papers from the train, came home at half past five, we sorted them out, then he did his round at Wethersfield American Air Force Base where my Aunty Audrey had been chopped up. He'd come back at lunchtime, flop on the settee, wake up in the early evening, watch telly still sprawled on it until late into the night until he fell asleep again, then get up at four. I can remember all the sofas we had because they were the old man's thrones of power. The first was a mammoth thing covered in grey velour. It weighed a ton, but at least it meant that it wasn't hurled around the sitting room. In the new house there was a sofa in cracked cream vinyl studded with five fat buttons. He would watch TV reclining on that sofa, wearing baggy tracksuits trousers. My mother moaned at him for not washing. He didn't eat meals in the dining room with us; instead, he ate lying down on the sofa, so one of us would be dispatched to take his food into his lair. I always dreaded it when she asked me to carry his dinner through. My mother would fetch his dirty dinner plate, come back out, hold up the knife and exclaim to us, 'Look! Clean! The knife's still clean!'

One day the old man had foraged through my bedroom, falling upon a couple of leftover *Forum* mags that I'd borrowed, and he exploded, haranguing me for taking these magazines. He was standing at the top of the stairs and had me pinioned against the wall. The stairs were open-tread, polished mahogany and very slippery. These shiny stairs were stretching away behind him and I thought, 'Yeah, one push, one good push.' I glanced over his shoulder and I braced.

He must have caught my intention because he muttered, 'I'll kill you . . .'

He owned a shotgun by this point. He walked around Pant Ken and the fourteen-acre field in a Barbour jacket, flat cap and Wellington boots. The only thing I can remember him shooting was a seagull. He bought two horses, for my mother and him to ride; they were huge black shire-horses, and my sister had two horses because she'd had an operation and the doctor had advised that riding would be good exercise for her. At one point she had three horses and I had a rusty old bike that was falling apart. The old man treated my sister differently; he never physically attacked her – I probably saw being a girl as a more acceptable way to win affection. So we had four horses, a couple of cats, a pair of springer spaniels and a beautiful shaggy dog called Maeve with hair the same colour as mine. We also had ducks, chickens, a rabbit and a goat, a bloody goat that was the most trouble.

The goat was there because of my mother's sentimental streak, she had seen an advert in the local paper: 'Baby goat for free. Otherwise it will be destroyed.' My mother brought home the kid, cooing, 'Oh! Isn't it cute!' not quite realising that a male kid would grow into a great beast that could drag me across the field if it wanted to. It was a handful, this goat, with its mad, keyhole eyes. I built it a wooden hut with a curtain across the door because goats hate the rain. It was a sturdy box that I could heave round the field, but it was weighty enough so that when I chained the goat to it, it wouldn't topple over. The box stayed in the same place for a few days while the goat ate a circle of grass round it, then I would roll the box across the field and he would eat another circle. I couldn't let the goat off the chain because it was a big, powerful beast and it would climb everything. The next-door neighbour was a little old lady who had taken her driving tests eleven times but still hadn't passed it. She was pulling out of the drive with her driving instructor when the goat *leapt* over the fence and jumped on to the bonnet of her car, utterly horrifying her. He was called Nuts because we had to have him de-nutted. I remember wrestling with the thing, holding it down when it was having its toenails cut. It strangled itself in the end on the chain, unfortunately.

Up the road from Pant Ken was an empty Victorian mansion with its own grounds within a walled garden where I used to walk the dogs. I stowed a bag of ladies' clothes I'd siphoned from the youth club jumble sale in this Victorian house and every so often I would go there on a quiet summer's afternoon to try on the women's clothes, then wander through the gardens of this derelict villa, feeling excited. I once found a gardener's mackintosh made from rubber and put that on too. Sometimes I would go there in the evening, dress up and amble in the moonlight. The grass was damp and dewy, and I was very aroused. They were raw moments.

I was tottering around the mansion one Sunday afternoon in this ensemble of women's clothes when I heard voices. It sounded like a family. I slunk into an overgrown summerhouse, crouched down and hid behind a pile of wood. Suddenly their dog bounced into the summerhouse and began sniffing me. I was whispering, 'Fack off! fack off!' to the Labrador because I was thinking any minute now they are going to come in here searching for their dog and find this seventeen-year-old boy dressed in an awful nylon dress and too-small stilettos. Eventually the dog wandered off, but I nearly pooped, not my pants, but somebody else's!

Getting up early every morning I'd see a lot of wildlife: foxes, owls and deer in the dawn. I would come home from school at six and take the dogs for a walk in the dark across the fields. I was never afraid of the dark. I saw a moonbow once. A moonbow is a rainbow cast not by the sun, but by a very bright full moon. Because there was very low light at night my eyes couldn't separate the colour into its parts, so I only saw a white rainbow: a moonbow. I caught sight of it walking the dogs across a stubble field and I wondered, 'What's that? That's amazing!'

Collage, 1983. Early work containing several examples of my personal iconography, crashed car, shed, pill box, pylon and girl with doll in Essex landscape

12

CHELMSFORD WAS QUITE
A HOT-BED OF PUNK

One Sunday morning I was delivering the newspapers when I saw the front cover of a supplement with a photograph of punks at a Sex Pistols concert. I was amazed by it, I thought, 'Fucking Hell! This is good!' I decided then and there I wanted to be a punk rocker. There were a lot of other boys at school who wanted to be punk rockers as well, one of whom became our hero because he was on the cover of the *Sunday Times Magazine* in a ripped school blazer. The headmaster was infuriated – a boy from King Edward the Sixth, in the school uniform, with safety pins!

The glorious amateurishness of punk meant that I could make my own outfit. I ripped the sleeves off a grey school shirt, then stencilled 'HATE' all over it with a home-made stencil. I bought plastic sandals, wore the school blazer covered in badges and put Vaseline in my hair. My pièce de résistance was from a bag of horse tack my brothers found in the loft that had been used to hobble carthorses to stop them running away. It was a huge horse collar with whopping great brass studs, very brutal-looking, that I wore round my neck, extremely proudly. It was massive. The downside was that it had three great big metal chain links attached to it so when I pogoed they used to smack me in the teeth.

Chelmsford was quite a hot-bed of punk. It had a lot of gigs to which my mum gave me a lift. I never drank or took drugs at gigs, I didn't have enough money. Instead, I put my heart and soul into being a pogoer, I used to go bonkers, getting extremely sweaty and adrenalised leaping up and down. When the Boomtown Rats played in Chelmsford, I was the best pogoer, so Bob Geldof hauled me on to the stage to dance, which was a proud moment for me. The Vibrators dragged me on stage because I was so mental it looked like I was having a seizure. That summer, a three-chord-wonder band called Crispy Ambulance played the Social Club at Chelmsford Football Ground and when the mosh pit became a sweat box, I pushed through the fire exit, sprinted out on to Chelmsford football pitch, in the centre of which was a colossal lawn sprayer, and raced round and round and round following the sprayer until I cooled off.

Chelmsford had a very healthy punk scene so, in the summer of 1977, a misguided person organised an all-day festival of punk at Chelmsford Football Club. I was excited, especially as The Damned were headlining and I put on my home-made punk outfit and the horse collar. I can remember the name of two bands that played and they were both atrocious. Bethnal were Prog-Rock but had realised punk was the future so punked themselves up and the Fruit-Eating Bears consisted of two guitarists with their legs as far apart as possible playing a single chord. Any group that wasn't hard-core punk, like reggae, was booed off. It was badly attended with a few people milling about at the front. And it was atmosphere-free; it became apparent halfway through that it was a big flop. When the scaffolding contractor who had built the stage realised he wasn't going to get paid, he shimmied to the top of the stage in the middle of one of the acts – and they were awful, awful acts – and started dismantling it, dropping heavy pieces of scaffolding into the well at the front while the band was playing. Then the police came on stage and arrested him in the middle of the set and the band kept thrashing, 'DRRRRRRRRRRRRRR!' The most punk thing of the whole day was that.

Punk was amazingly refreshing and gloriously amateur. I loved the home-madeness, the aesthetic of the record covers and the fanzines, and the combination of daftness and scariness. Before punk, I'd never seen anyone with a Mohican or blue hair, and pierced ears seemed exotic to me. Early punks looked like I looked: a Sixth Former in his school blazer with a few badges, a school tie at half mast and slightly messy hair, even early Joy Division look like Sixth Formers.

I listened to punk rock and heavy metal on Radio Caroline, a pirate radio station off the East Coast, and went a couple of times to the Radio Caroline Road Show in Braintree. The entertainment consisted of DJs playing air guitar on stage – or air organ when the organ solos came on – along with the audience. Every so often they would put a ghastly chart hit on a chopping block, then hack the record up in front of the baying crowd. It was funny and it was a chance to get sweaty and do youth culture.

My sister had started going to the local youth club and I went with her once a month to the Friday night disco where boys and girls, all with a Coco-Cola and KitKat, huddled at opposite ends of the hall. We both loved the disco and – despite being a punk rocker – it rapidly became the most exciting thing in my life because I enjoyed dancing and it was the height of disco. The disco in the town hall played chart hits, with a couple of smooch numbers to establish relationships, some rock'n'roll, a Heavy Metal record, back to disco and smooch numbers at the end. During 'Once, Two, Three Times a Lady', I went for a girl from the village called Hilary and we snogged – she had braces on her teeth. I fancied her so we used to go to the local playground and canoodle, until we started doing a lot of babysitting together, which was an opportunity for a free settee to spoon on while earning a bit of money at the same time. We used to spend many hours snogging and fondling – nothing more – to Roy Orbison on a velour sofa. One night one of the kids came downstairs while we were lying there in the nude. Years later I found out from the parents, 'Yes, he remembered that.'

During the skateboarding craze, I found being a rural skateboarder was very frustrating as there was no smooth concrete in the village. The first time I saw a skateboard my friend was riding one around the village. I asked him what it was. He told me and said, 'I bought it off a bloke at the American Air Force Base.' I immediately went to Chelmsford and bought the cheapest possible plastic skateboard and became obsessed. Then, a few months later, when I had saved enough money from my paper round tips, I made a special trip on my own to London to buy a good-quality skateboard. Even though Chelmsford was near London, it seemed very far away and I had only been there twice before on tourist trips with the school, but I desperately wanted a cool skateboard.

The most thrilling experience on my new skateboard was skating down a very steep hill into the centre of Bardfield. At night gangs of us gathered at the top of that hill before bolting down it like a shot, straight across the T-junction and, when we were going fast enough, up and over the hump-backed bridge. Then we dared each other to go down the hill again, this time backwards, lying down or holding hands. Once I'd passed running speed, I couldn't jump off because I would fall over but in those days if I fell over I just bounced.

There was the frustration of there being very little to do in the village. To while away the time we lolled around the local bus stop egging one another on to jump on the car roof of the gay couple who owned the pub to taunt them, or daring each other to drive around the village green on a moped in the nude, or in underpants, because naked would be going just too far. Once we grabbed the smallest boy and hung him over the edge of the church tower so he could put the village clock back an hour. We were bored. I remember consciously thinking about the lads I was fraternising with, 'Fucking hell, these are thick people! God! I'm bored!' and if I used a word with more than two syllables they'd say, 'What? You swallowed the dictionary, or something?' But they were the local company so when I wasn't playing with my brothers at home, I hung out with ordinary lads. Now I look at the boys lingering in the square in front of my house and remember, 'I was there once and I was bored shitless.' One night someone had the idea of holding a steeplechase down the back gardens of a row of houses, leaping over the hedges. We must have been tipsy. One of the hedges was a thorn bush; I was still picking thorns out of my knee two years later. Other times we'd be lolloping down the lane to the youth club when a car would come along, so we'd all pretend to be having a terrible punch-up and it looked like they were driving past a horrible fight. Then, when the car pulled to a halt, we would scoff, 'Yeah . . . ?' I was out at night and feeling mischievous because I'd had half a lager. We all went to the pub at fifteen because the pub was happy for our custom. I was once in the pub when the barman asked me, 'How old are you, then?' and I said, 'I'm sixteen!'

The last bus out of the village was at six o'clock in the evening so the boys in the village were obsessed with motorbikes because they were a ticket out of Bardfield. Several of them had Yamaha Fizzy mopeds. We used to career from one rural pub to another and sip a half of lager in each one. The only topic of conversation in the pub was who saw sparks fly when they scraped their footrest going round the corner and who definitely saw eighty miles an hour on their speedometer. At the end of the summer when I was eighteen, I announced to my mum, 'I've got two hundred and fifty quid saved up from my job. I'm going to buy a motorbike today.'

She answered, 'You can't just go and buy a motorbike, it's not like buying a packet of fags or something.'

I said, 'Yes you can.' I looked in the small ads, found a suitable one, a Suzuki GT 125, mum drove me to Chelmsford and a very nice gentleman showed me his bike. I didn't know anything about bikes but it seemed all right so I bought it.

He asked, 'Have you ever ridden a motorbike before?' He let me have a go around his back garden and I drove it into a rosebush. And ploughed up his flowerbed. 'You're not driving that home, are you?' he asked.

I wanted a full-face crash helmet but my mother insisted, 'You don't want to spend all that money on a crash helmet!' so I got the cheapest one I could buy, an open-faced polycarbonate helmet, which was fourteen pounds. I didn't have proper bike kit or a leather jacket either because I couldn't afford it. Instead, I borrowed a sheepskin coat from my mother. I spent a whole day swapping the buttonholes round from the left- to the right-hand side. I ruined the jacket – sheepskin was the most impossible material to try to sew and the jacket gaped and leaked ever more – but I was paranoid about appearing to wear a woman's jacket.

13

A FOREIGN WORLD I
WAS ENTERING

The first thought that struck me when I started Foundation Course was, 'Oh God, Art lessons are full time now.' Suddenly I was at Braintree College of Further Education on a forty-hour art-making week, whereas at school I'd spent eight hours a week, at most, making art. I thought, 'I'm going to do art, all day, every day now' and I treated the Foundation Course like a job.

Braintree, which I thought was an amazing name, was nine miles from Bardfield and once vilified for having the ugliest people in the country. The college had a very small Foundation Course with thirty students in a year, all straight from school, doing the one-year course to decide which branch of art they would specialise in at art college. Mickey Green, who ran the Foundation, was striking-looking with his big, round, David Hockney glasses and his colourful, stripy seer-sucker blazer. He was a sixties arty person with a geezerish vibe, from what I thought of as the School of the Denim Shirt with a Bit of Grey Chest Hair Poking Out. He had Swinging Sixties London culture mixed with a sprinkling of *Guardian*-reading progressiveness. Probably screwed one of the students. There was an overlapping of values, bohemian yet still vulnerable to the vagaries of male competitiveness.

I wanted Mickey's approval and I immediately made work that would please him. I practically did his work: I made a blobby red painting with, 'HEY YOU!' slap in the middle, a Pop Art piece, like a Ruscha, which was exactly the style of work Mickey did. I was seeking his approval. I even said to Mickey, 'Have you done much work lately? Well, don't worry, I'm doing your work for you,' rather arrogantly, aged eighteen.

The focus of the Foundation was to get students on to a degree course. In the winter term we had a taste of everything: printing, photography, fashion and graphics, drawing, a lot of life drawing, and many exercises with colour and technique. At the end of that first term each student put on a small display of work, which Mickey studied then proclaimed, 'Well! You're definitely a photographer!' Or, 'Yes! You're a sculptor and you're going off to this college.' As for me, Mickey told me, 'Oh yes! You're a painter.'

The Foundation Course was about pulling us away from doing very detailed pictures of cars, bombers, or girls' tits, which was what I drew. My art teacher at school had said, 'Sex has been an inspiration to artists throughout the ages, Grayson, but it can get in the way.' He was referring to a drawing I was doing of a woman, a very scantily clad woman, with a crossbow, leaning against a tree and in the background was an *enormously* phallic car with a bonnet three blocks long, and she was legs akimbo.

'Why, Grayson darling . . .'

I think he saw it and thought, 'Oh, hormones.' Mickey was also battling against students coming straight from school, being overly neat, obsessive and worried about 'doing the right thing', so in order to counteract that he offered us the template of the roaring wine, women and song Augustus-John-artist, who drew with his dick. The teachers had an outmoded idea that an artist had to be loose, expressive and free. It was a cliché that came out of American Expressionism, of the passionate, animalistic artist who was macho and manly, dictatorially stating: 'THIS IS WHAT ART *IS*!'

Mickey encouraged us to keep a sketchbook in which to be random, experimental and free. Often my sketchbooks were what Mickey liked best. I was an adept draughtsman yet it wasn't an ability I used much. Instead, I made splodgy, abstract work and another Pop Art piece, a wooden Marmite label. I did an extremely detailed drawing of a spaceship interior. It was bad and Mickey attacked it for being obsessive, although obsessive neatness is one of the main forces in my work now. The Foundation Course was a time of loosening up when I realised anything could go, so I tried a bit of everything but at the same time I was always tied to my own ideas. No matter how free you feel, you are only as good as your ideas.

The first object I made in pottery was a skateboarding trophy, which blew up in the kiln. I later made an awful blob thing, a globule of clay that looked like tree roots, which my mother used to have sitting on the top shelf in the kitchen. The neighbour in Bardfield asked to borrow it, saying, 'That will make a lovely vase to put a flower arrangement in.'

On Foundation there were students from many different backgrounds. Foundation was a foreign world that I was entering. I was seeing into a freer, more adult, middle-class world where culture was important in people's lives. Even though I had been to a very selective state school, the majority of lads there were Ordinary Joes and educationally I hadn't been in the company of girls for the last seven years. I was so shy at first, so non-verbal, that two girls, Jane and Diana, thought I was German. Diana was posh and Jane was middle-class and attractive, so I began hanging out with them. One night I went to Diana's house and we all ended up on the bed cuddling, which, for me, was immensely charged but I wasn't sure how to handle it, being very young and innocent in these things. Diana made a pass at me, so I started seeing Diana. I was still dating Hilary and both relationships overlapped for a while. Eventually Hilary and I fizzled out, probably because of my appalling behaviour – I had no concept of integrity in relationships.

Diana lived just beyond the boundary of our newspaper round in a nearby village in a higgledy-piggledy manor house. The metal fireback in the kitchen had '1386' moulded in it and the windows were so old that they were thicker at the bottom of the pane than the top because glass, being a liquid, slowly moves downwards. Her father was about six foot nine, ex-Navy, with a terribly-terribly booming voice. He worked for the East India Company: Diana was born in Rajastan and talked about her Indian nanny. It was totally different from my family: very exotic, very posh, utterly foreign, with lovely antique furniture and an Aga in the kitchen. I must have seemed like a bit of rough and ready, stepping out of my house that had wonky MFI furniture that I was forever screwing back together because it was always wonking about, then going to this manor house with fabulously inlaid writing desks and shelves crammed with books, paintings on the wall and Oriental carpets on the floor, all owned by an impressive, super-tall dad whose size eighteen shoes were like boats lined up in the hallway. He had to stoop because the ceilings were so low and I thought, 'Why is he living in a house like this? Why isn't he in a nice Georgian house with tall ceilings?'

The mother was only five foot three. She was quite a dragon; there was always a slight bitterness to her. Diana's sister was a potter and had her own pottery in an outhouse. She used to come in from the pottery, freezing cold, covered in mud and I thought, 'What an awful job.' She was very much a rustic-style potter who worked on a wheel and built massive wood-firing kilns in the garden, sitting up through the night to look after the kiln. It all seemed a lot of work to me. It was the first relationship I had where it was exciting because of my girlfriend's family and her social circle. It was exciting too because Diana was beautiful, pale with big lips, a strong-looking woman. She dressed chaotically, but if she wore the right clothes she could look fabulous.

After a day at college I would have my tea at home at six o'clock, then have supper at the manor house with good wine; Diana's father had a superb cellar so I was introduced to fine wine. They indulged me, although once when the mother found me lying on Diana's bed – we weren't having sex but certainly we were heavy petting – she was outraged and didn't want me in Diana's bedroom any more.

Over the year Diana and I became proper girl- and boyfriend. I would go to her house and we went for walks. I lost my virginity with Diana; we had been working up to it in various stages. Her parents were away for the day and *Life on Earth* was on TV. We went into her parents' quarters, a lovely old room in this fourteenth-century manor, and her dad, being six foot nine, had a *big* bed. Sex was awkward and slightly disappointing. I found the mechanics of it quite hard to do, but I managed it, thinking, 'Well, that's that!' We got better at it as we went along. I must have enjoyed sex because in subsequent months and years I took an awful lot of trouble criss-crossing the country, chasing various women to get it.

Soon after I lost my virginity Diana and I rode on my motorbike to my father's wedding. Diana was looking particularly gorgeous and my dad was very struck by her. He had divorced Maureen-Ann – I think her rages became too much for him – and he was marrying Pippa, the next-door neighbour who had come with her husband and children on that fateful holiday to the caravan park with us.

Mad Kid's Bedroom Wall

This was the third wife. He moved three doors down – he wasn't very adventurous in his search for women.

It was imperative that I got into a proper art college after the foundation year because art was my ticket out of Essex – the pot *Mad Kid's Bedroom Wall* is about escaping my roots through art. I imagined myself as carrying on to become a painter or a sculptor. Braintree had an almost one hundred per cent record for getting students on to a degree course and was paranoid that you went to the right college, the one you *could* get into. The London art colleges were the best, although Central was an unobtainable pinnacle. Chelsea and Hornsey were the crème de la crème; a couple of the northern ones had a sound reputation too. I didn't dare apply to a London college; I wasn't going to waste my chance on an establishment I didn't think I could get into. I liked the sound of Portsmouth Poly; it had a free-and-easy reputation. I didn't want to go to the north – that was scary territory – but Portsmouth was well regarded yet was still a long way from Essex.

In May of 1979 I went for my interview for Portsmouth. Sean, a friendly ex-Braintree student, put me up for the night in his digs and we watched the election results; he had a felt pen and was drawing on the TV screen over the top of Mrs Thatcher. We went down to the town hall in the Guildhall Square to hear the final results and I was daunted by Portsmouth because it seemed like a vast city with soaring tower blocks. It wasn't a big city, it was a small city, but it was a lot bigger than Chelmsford.

By chance Sean was the student on the interview panel the next day. I laid out my work and the interview went perfectly well. Afterwards Sean came out, looked at me and announced, 'You've got in. There wasn't any doubt about you,' which meant I didn't have to wait for the letter, I knew straight away.

So I went home jolly. I thought, 'Maybe I should have tried for a flashier college,' but I was happy I had been accepted at Portsmouth.

I thought I was OK as an artist. I knew I was able but I had no sense that I was especially gifted. I don't think a gift is apparent at nineteen in a contemporary artist. Contemporary art demands a voice, though few artists have found their voice at nineteen. What is apparent in young work is technical skill – Raphael drew like an angel at fifteen – as well as an aptitude for the more physical aspects of the work, but the voice and the emotional intelligence come later. I didn't have that and my work was very derivative. I don't think it was peculiar that nobody thought that I would do well in the art world and it was probably better for me than if I had been pumped up as a good artist. I was an average art student bumbling on.

Later, in my final year at art college, when I was the student on the interview panel I thought it would be obvious who was good, who was bad and who was a genius, but it wasn't. There was little difference between a good applicant who was admitted and a bad one who wasn't. 'Do we want this person in our college?' and 'Are they committed?' were more important considerations than whether their art was good. It certainly wasn't apparent that there was a genius being interviewed, their work wasn't developed enough and it was *always* thoroughly copyist.

Grayson on the Foundation Course

The grant system for college was means tested so if you came from a well-off family your parents contributed a portion of your upkeep. I knew my stepfather wasn't going to give me any money whatsoever. The form asked for details of your parents' income, so I put the bald facts on the application: 'I don't know. I wouldn't be able to find out and even if he earned enough to support me, there's no way he'd give me any money.' I got a full grant.

After I'd got into art college, the old man took me aside in the garage stating, 'I don't want you to come back after you've gone to college. I don't want you back in this house.' I was upset by that and trudged off for a moody walk. After I left I never did sleep another night there.

14

ONE OF THOSE ECCENTRIC JOBS YOU ONLY EVER DO AS A STUDENT

Great fields of sugar beet are grown in East Anglia and in the summer of 1978 when I was eighteen and had just finished my A levels, I got a crappy job working at a sugar beet factory in Essex. My first task was to sit in a digger cab next to a deep pit where they settled all the topsoil that was washed off the sugar beet. The soil was dug out again and the factory sold it back to the farmers! The management thought the lorry drivers were fiddling the company by saying they had pulled out more loads of soil than they had, so it was my responsibility to count the number of loads: count lorry, tick, count lorry, tick, one lorry drive past, tick, a mind-numbing chore. I sat in the digger cab all day long reading whatever was on the shelf at work, which were Jane Eyre and *The Pan Book of Horror Stories*.

I was very quickly promoted to assisting the industrial

chemist, a tottery old gent who had worked there for decades. Our task was to test the sugar. Every morning I collected a bag of sugar as it came off the production line and we analysed it in various ways: sieved it, passed light through it and mixed it with chemicals to test it for impurities and grain size. Sometimes we did odd jobs, one of which was cleaning the desalination plant where there was a giant tank of caustic soda. The chemist said, 'We've got to clean this tank so first of all bucket the water out.' A thick layer of caustic soda had settled at the bottom with a layer of water on top. I didn't know what caustic soda was so I started bucketing out the water. This tank was six feet high; I could have fallen into it quite easily and dissolved. As soon as I started emptying it, the solution was being stirred up, so the water in my bucket was gradually getting stronger and stronger with alkali. I had no goggles, no gloves. As I slopped it across the floor I was spilling it on my shoes: I only had one pair, which were the blue suede shoes I wore everywhere. I looked down to see a pool of blue dye seeping out of them and when I stepped forward the upper came off the sole of my shoe! My feet were red, so the chemist said, 'I think you better go to the nurse.' The nurse checked my feet to make sure the company wasn't going to be sued. I had red feet for a couple of days.

After that I was terrified of acids and alkalis. We had to handle powerful acids and alkalis a lot in the chemistry lab and I thought, 'Christ Almighty, who am I working with here? This idiot!' He got a proper telling off about it. He might have been British Bowls Champion at the time, but he was a doddery fool. It was one of those eccentric jobs you only ever do as a student.

Being a sugar factory where zillions of tonnes of sugar were stored, there was a constant problem with wasps. Wasps made their nests in the grounds, then zoomed in on the sugar: there were swarms of them hovering in the factory. There were jumbo insecticutors at the doors of the factory that went VCHKUFF-VCHKUFF-KUFF-KUFF the whole time. Employees were paid a pound if they found a wasp nest so the workers would spend their lunchtimes careering around the grounds after a wasp to find its nest in the hope of earning a few extra quid.

The following summer, after my Foundation Course and before I went to art college, I worked in a dog biscuit factory. Leftover bread from the Mother's Pride bakery would be brought by the lorry-load to the factory and dumped into a colossal pile, where it stayed until it went stale. A team of women spent all day sitting at a conveyor belt separating the bread from its plastic bags and wire fastenings, then it was thrown into an enormous gas-powered dryer which tumble-dried the bread until it shrivelled hard. Finally it was crushed into dog biscuits, cattle feed and fish bait.

I was general humper in the factory. All day long I hauled hundredweight sacks of cattle food around – which was hard graft – loading up thirty-five-tonne lorries with sacks of cattle feed. I was immediately allowed, with no training, to drive the fork-lift truck. The floor was wet and slippery so the truck – this heavy, unwieldy vehicle that could crush people – would spin around out of control. One day I backed the fork-lift truck into the time clock and wrenched it off the wall. They were a jovial bunch, in a dilapidated factory that was constantly breaking down; there was always a fire breaking out or someone was getting their fingers chopped off in the shredder. The company had a sideline breeding worms for anglers. They had a pump joined to the mains, out of which raw sewage flowed and the women stood all day sorting the worms out of a mixture of sewage and manure, which is what the worms lived off. The foreman who ran the worm farm collected the used condoms out of the sewage, then had them hanging up in a row in his office like a score chart of the day. It was a funny job, but it earned me enough money to buy a motorbike.

15

REPOSITORY FOR KEEPING
HIS WHOLE SELF ACTIVE

Henry Darger, who died in 1973, spent his entire life writing and illustrating his masterwork called *The Story of the Vivian Girls, in What Is Known as the Realms of the Unreal, of the Glandeco-Angelinian War Storm, Caused by the Child Slave Rebellion*. The story was set on a vast, alien planet that had the earth for its moon and told the adventures of seven Catholic girls called the Vivian Princesses who led a child slave rebellion against the adults, which prompted the Glandeco-Angelinian War Storm. Darger appears in several guises in the story as Henry Dargarus, in good and bad forms. Many of the children are nude; curiously, a lot of the girls have penises. At first Darger was considered a suppressed paedophile, although now the theory is that he identified with the children, that they represent his childish, innocent part, hence his gravestone reads 'Henry Darger, Artist and Protector of Children'.

In the summer of 1979 I chugged up to London from Braintree with Mickey in his 2CV – this was when it was still feasible to drive into London – to visit 'The Outsiders', an exhibition of Art Brut at the Hayward Gallery. I was astounded by what I saw. I learned that Art Brut was created by spontaneous, untrained artists who made art outside the art world. It had Adolf Wölfli who was one of the most famous Outsider artists, but the artist I remembered best was Henry Darger. There were some of his violent paintings with children being massacred by soldiers. I read the blurb, thought, 'Oh God, this is *really* spooky' and was shocked.

Darger was born in Chicago in 1892. When his mother died in childbirth four years later his father, a disabled tailor, put him in an orphanage. Later on he was placed in a children's mental asylum; the diagnosis was masturbation. He grew up in the asylum having a dreadful time, escaping when he was sixteen, walking across country and living rough. He returned to Chicago where he got work as a janitor in a Catholic hospital, a job he stayed in all

Henry Darger, '*Trapped in lighted cavern they*

his life. He was a very reclusive character who had hardly any friends or, as far as is known, had a relationship with a woman. He was obsessively religious, unfailingly going to church three times every day. He never showed his art, his art didn't leave his apartment until he was dead. He's an Outsider Artist because he had no training, and he is the purest and most unsullied kind of Outsider because he wasn't exposed to collectors and exhibitions. His landlord, who cleared out his flat when he died, was a photographer, so recognised what he had discovered and didn't destroy it, which could so easily have happened. There was an element of Salieri and Mozart to it. I wonder what it must have been like for a middling photographer-illustrator to find out that the hermetic old man who was his tenant was a brilliantly talented artist?

Most of the figures are carbon-traced from children's comics, Darger didn't think he was a very good draughtsman and so he adapted found illustrations. There are

try to elude the Glandelinians surrounding them'

explosions, forest fires and landscapes collaged into the pictures. The composition and colour are astonishing. His sense of colour is astounding. The writing in his opus was articulate and his vocabulary mature.

Darger is the artist I identify with most in terms of his creative pathways. I feel a kindred spirit with how his imagination worked, the way he sought refuge in a fantasy world in the same way that I secreted my imagination and artistic practice into a shed where I retreated to do my work in an enclosed, secure environment while observing the world. I see in Henry Darger's work that the real world was too painful to bear, so he made an alternative. *The Story of the Vivian Girls* was a metaphor for his internal, emotional life. I identify with how Darger used to commentate out loud as he was drawing. His landlord, overhearing voices, yelled, 'No visitors allowed!' to which Darger replied, 'There's no one in here!' Then the landlord heard him scolding his imaginary people, 'I *told* you not to talk so loudly.'

Getting attention is a large part of making art. Getting attention is a powerful inducement to change or keep certain styles and ideas. Take the fact that I make vases and my vases were well received, which has been a strong motivation to continue creating them. If I were Henry Darger making art for myself I might change this or move that without being aware of art history or what the outside world thinks of it or wants. He chose the style, the content and the format solely to fit in with his needs as an artist, for himself only. What Darger represents to me is that pure artistic drive.

The idea of Art Brut, of not being aware of the art

world, appealed to me. At the time I didn't have these thoughts, I merely soaked in 'The Outsiders' exhibition to the extent that my drawings over the following three years were heavily informed by Henry Darger, but subconsciously. If you'd asked me at nineteen 'Whom are you copying?' I wouldn't have been able to say. The artists whom I would have said I liked were the German Neo-Expressionists, Kiefer, A.R. Penck, Baselitz and Joseph Beuys particularly. I just held the images of Darger's work in my mind. I didn't see them or any reference to them again or know where I could possibly find them. I couldn't even remember his name. I biked to the Art Brut museum in Switzerland with my wife in the late eighties looking for Darger's work but they didn't have any: now there is a whole room there dedicated to him. He has become the most sought-after and collected Outsider Artist. Paintings by him sell for $60,000. Darger is the nearest we have to an undiscovered genius in late twentieth-century art and of all the artists I know of, he has the most romantic story.

It was some years later that I came across Darger again and I was very moved. By then I was in therapy, thinking about the nature of psychotherapy and working on the first vase I made on this theme. I was searching for a set of metaphorical images that exactly matched what I wanted to say about looking back at one's childhood. In 2000 I made a pot called *The Revenge of the Alison Girls* – I misremembered the Vivian Girls as the Alison Girls – decorated with nude Alison Girls herding up parents into concentration camps, then executing them. I was describing the pot to someone when they told me, 'Henry Darger drew the Vivian Girls. He's just had a big show at the Folk Museum in New York.'

I identify with the comfort and escape Darger found in creating a parallel universe. He played out himself through all the characters in his story, which meant he was able to be whole in his imaginary world: it was a repository for keeping his whole self active. I am touched by the survival mechanism he used all his life, which I used with my games and models until I was about fifteen. It was as if I was in a prison while my imagination was the exercise yard, and I allowed all the parts of myself to go out into that imaginary world to be themselves.

Darger did art therapy in his way, a wonderfully spontaneous mode of self-psychiatric medication. And I did it in my way: I played it out with Alan Measles. What has made me an artist – and kept me intact as a child – were the channels whereby I turned a feeling into a metaphor. I went through puberty while this mechanism was still operating, so a lot of my erotic imagination was drawn into it too.

I still use those well-worn corridors to this day, in that I experience the world, allow it to stew, then I find a way of putting it out there in the simplistic language of pottery. Pottery is not a very effective way of conveying complex thoughts, so I have to communicate what I hope are diverse ideas within the limited vocabulary of ceramics. Henry Darger's illustrations are so powerful that people get their message within a few moments of looking at his art. This, for me, is the crux of why I'm an artist. It's not in the detail of the picture; it is in the atmosphere of the world you enter. I haven't taken being an artist seriously enough through my life: I am starting to do it more now. I haven't thanked the art world enough for what it has done for me.

16

'DON'T COPY WHAT'S FASHIONABLE NOW, COPY WHAT'S GOING TO BE FASHIONABLE IN TWO YEARS' TIME'

In the autumn of 1979 the day came for me to leave home. I piled all my belongings – of which I had hardly any – into a black bin liner, strapped it on to the back of the Suzuki, taped a map of the south-west to the petrol tank and phut-phut-phutted from Bardfield to art college. Halfway there I got trapped on a roundabout by the M11 realising that every turn-off was a motorway, worrying, 'Fuck! How did I get here? I'm not allowed on any of these roads.' I was only a learner with L-plates. I decided, 'Sod it! I'm going on the M11.' I ripped off the L-plates, got on the motorway and eventually spluttered to a halt outside my landlady's in Portsmouth. She was incredibly thin, she smoked and she cooked nondescript meals. She had a son in the Marines and a not very good wardrobe.

I don't think I ever saw her eat and I was there until the following June.

I didn't want to spend any time in my lodgings. Instead, for my first term I hung out with Chris Cheshire and Greg Palmer. They were from the north. I hadn't met people from the north before. I don't know what they thought of me; I practically stalked them. I was round their room in the halls of residence *every* evening, desperately lonely, but I wouldn't have admitted it. They probably got annoyed with me. I used to turn up at their room every single night, sit there joking and japing until very late because I could *not* spend time with my anorexic landlady at the other end of town.

I was very thin too. I weighed ten stone but, unlike my landlady, I had a voracious appetite. Every morning I ate a full English breakfast, a cake for elevenses, then pie, beans and double chips for lunch in the student dining room. I had a snack in the afternoon followed by a full roast dinner at the landlady's at six. Later on, after I'd hung around at the halls of residence, I polished off sausages and chips from the chip shop on the way home. I had a huge amount of energy; I never got tired, I was ticking over very fast, at twenty thousand revs.

My artwork in my first year at college was *awful*. I made some of the worst things I have ever made. It was dreadful because two forces were still operating within me: I treated art like work, it was something I did, like school or the dog biscuit factory, and I also wanted to please my lecturers to the extent that I made pastiches of their work. Furthermore, the college had Terry, the ineffective pottery technician who was supposed to assist the students, although every piece of pottery I ever gave him to fire came back broken or the wrong colour. I would indicate, 'I want this piece to come out jet black, Terry,' but instead it would turn beige. An art college tip is probably the repository for some of the ugliest objects on earth because they aren't only ugly objects, they're ugly objects that are trying to be art.

Every week one or two visiting lecturers would give a talk, then spend the day with the students. Nicholas Pope spoke about his mum bringing him cups of tea in the shed while he was working and his sweet, gentle way of talking about his art appealed to me. The influences of the artist Anish Kapoor and the sculptor Edward Allington could soon be seen filtering through the students' work. I saw Anish Kapoor's work for the first time at an opening of hip young sculptors at the ICA in the summer of 1980. It was a pile of pigment that I desperately wanted to touch to discover if it was solid or merely a mound of powder. In the same show Antony Gormley exhibited a double mattress sculpted from sliced bread with people-shaped holes bitten out of it. Edward Allington sculpted sizeable plaster blobs so within a few weeks of his lecture there was a rash of plaster lumps, an appeal of plaster being that, along with wax and fibreglass, it was a free material. In the early eighties an artist called Larry Knee built a Gothic artefact that looked like a miniature version of the Albert Memorial decorated with fragments of teeth, bottles, clock mechanisms, broken china dollies and scraps of iron and silverware, all of which he unearthed in Victorian landfills. He came to speak to us and I was very influenced by him.

The Head of the Department was a Francophile who led an annual student trip to Paris. I hadn't been abroad before. I had some money left over from working in the dog biscuit factory so I decided, 'I'm going to go abroad.' I took a *huge* suitcase stuffed with all my clothes but I didn't wear any of them apart from a change of underpants. All I wore the whole time was jeans, a T-shirt and my leather jacket even though I had five changes of clothes. There was one cool boy called Ryan who, when he got on the boat, only had one small plastic bag containing three pairs of underpants and two T-shirts, which was his entire luggage for the whole week. I had this mammoth suitcase that weighed a ton and I got searched at customs going out *and* coming back. I've learned since that if I've got a favourite look I'm going to wear it all the time.

While crossing the Channel I copped off with Jen Mortimer, an art student in the year above me. We started snogging as soon as we boarded the ferry and we became a couple during the trip. Jen and I spent our time in Paris eating at no-frills restaurants, drinking plastic bottles of discount wine and looking at a lot of art. We were staying in a student hostel and, despite the boys' dormitory offering no privacy, Jen spent one night with me in my bunk bed. When we got back Jen discarded the boyfriend she'd had since her Foundation Course, who had moved to Portsmouth to be with her. I was still seeing Diana so every other weekend I would trundle across the southwest on the train to Falmouth where Diana was at art college in the hope of getting five minutes when we were alone – she had three flatmates – to have sex.

Very soon into my relationship with Jen I was lying in

bed with her when I announced, 'Jen . . . Jen . . . I've. Got. Something. To. Tell. You. I . . . AM . . . A . . . TRANSVESTITE.' She burst out laughing, not about me being a transvestite but over the formality with which I told her. It was my emotion and seriousness in confiding it to her that she found hilarious. Jen mocked me mercilessly over it. Although it was cruel of her to laugh, I took it on the chin because I was besotted with her and she was so much fun. I was very earnest about dressing up because transvestism was a large aspect of myself that I was allowing out of the closet and, for me, it was very erotic – perhaps Jen was slightly uncomfortable with that. It would be a while before she saw me wearing women's clothing.

Jen and her flatmate Veronica helped me piece together a haphazard wardrobe from Oxfam and advised me on my make-up. Veronica had a higgledy-piggledy heap of wigs from jumble sales that she was using to make an artwork and among that heap I found a wig for myself that was vaguely serviceable. Then, one afternoon when the landlady was out I sneaked into her room to try on some of her dresses. She had snazzy seventies clothes in polyester that I couldn't resist, but unfortunately she was a small size; we were both thin, but she was *really* thin. I don't know if she knew what I'd done, but after that her bedroom door was locked. Nevertheless I began having surreptitious dressing-up sessions in my room, taking photographs of myself in women's clothing. The lecturers had said that a camera was an essential tool for an artist so I bought an extremely cheap, third-rate SLR, a Zenith, which enabled me to take my first photograph of Claire, an important moment for me as a trannie. Claire was me in a bad frock looking nervously into the lens. I wasn't sure if I was Grayson or Claire in the dress: many things, 'Claire' and 'transvestite' included, didn't exist until they had a name.

I was spending every evening with Jen and Veronica in their flat, where the record collection, the clothes, the jokes, were all in inverted commas, everything was once

Earliest photo of me in women's clothes, 1979

removed slightly. It was an environment which asked, 'Dare I take anything seriously?' because Jen and Veronica would pounce on me if I did. It was an extremely creative ambience because it meant I questioned what I was doing until it stood up to a very rigorous test of their acerbic wit. I revelled in the masquerade of us being cruel to each other. Nor were we frightened of being naff, which was being prepared to be unstylish and old-fashioned in order to be personally expressive – naff became a strong force in my creativity. We dared to be uncool but we were uncool in a way we knew would be cool in a few months' or years' time. The painter Martin Maloney used to say to students, 'Don't copy what's fashionable now, copy what's going to be fashionable in two years' time.' That was a dictum I began to follow then.

The big event for Jen, Veronica and me was the Students Union disco. Portsmouth didn't have hip nightclubs so the best night out on a Friday was the students' regular, to which even the trendies from town turned up. Trendy meant post-punk. New Romanticism was emerging; people were dressing up. The three of us spent every weekend voraciously foraging through jumble sales and charity shops in a quest for eccentric clothes to pose in at the disco. I didn't go public with my transvestism in that first year so I wore men's clothes, Lurex shirts and dinner jackets, and launched into dressing up, revelling in the attention it brought me.

Jen's elder sister, Fiona, arrived from London for a Friday night disco wearing a skin-tight pink mohair trouser suit and, with her white hair, she looked like a young Mary Peters. She was a dynamo, a combination of a Girl Guide – she was like a Brown Owl – a clubbing butterfly and a bit of a rocker. Fiona had an astonishing wardrobe and was an excellent dresser in the most curious way. I would ask her, 'Where did you get that outfit?'

She would reply, 'They have a jumble sale at St Martin's Fashion School of all the designs that got rejected.' Once she found a big roll of corrugated paper in a skip, wrapped it round herself lots of times, tied it on with a yellow scarf, then went nightclubbing in a roll of pink paper. This was an eye opener to me, influencing the way I was dressing. Fiona was very good-looking, very striking and absolutely full of life, the best dancer I'd ever seen – not technically, but the most enthusiastic. When the worst records came on and nobody else would dance, Fiona, Jen, Veronica and I liked to monopolise the dance floor, showing off and larking around. Fiona was the first person I knew who liked Abba in a postmodern way. They were at the tail end of their success, but Fiona, before they'd even come to an end, was being ironic about them, enthusing, 'Wow! ABBA! Oh, I love ABBA!' which was uncool because everybody else was raving about punk rock. Abba was in opposition to punk. The flip I got from the sisters was to kick against the pricks, twist things round and say, 'This could be funny if we just turn it over.'

On Saturday nights we went to gigs. We saw Black Sabbath, Motorhead and groovy groups like The Cure and The Human League. Local bands had cheap or free gigs, all very poorly attended; the audience would be hugging the back wall of the room while supping a pint. Most local groups were shockingly bad but we nevertheless decided, 'We are going to make a great big effort.'

The three of us dolled up, got bladdered on cheap, student promo – usually Pernod – and threw ourselves into being the band's biggest fans, dancing very passionately right at the front. Some bands took us at face value, believing we idolised them, sometimes even inviting us up on to the stage to sing along with them, which delighted us and was a triumph, our apotheosis, or else they got extremely annoyed and told us, 'Piss off!' There was an atrocious, long-haired Heavy Metal band called Zeus whom we adored, for whom Jen would dress in the complete Heavy Metal look. One night she won their head-banging competition and was given a Zeus T-shirt with 'ZEUS WORLD TOUR' on the front and a map of Portsmouth on the back with a list of three pubs.

At the end of my first year I very swiftly made, in one afternoon, a curious little ceramic sculpture that looked as if it were an ethnic object. It was peculiar in that it appeared to be a cross between a gutted fish and a boat. I fired it in the raw clay, then painted it with a blood-red and grey interior. It had a wigwam roof decorated to look like sheepskin and supported on sticks. The Institute of Contemporary Art had an annual survey show of student art called 'The New Contemporaries', which had a history of well-known artists who had exhibited in it as their first showing and in 1980 I entered a slide of this piece. To my surprise it was accepted.

17

'OH. DO YOU WORK ON A FARM?'

When Jen and I first arrived at Fiona's squat in the summer of 1980, 'Princess Julia', a glamorous, gay, breathtakingly beautiful woman glided down the stairs, looked me up and down, and asked, 'Oh. Do you work on a farm?' because I had a brown corduroy suit on, a ruddy face and

Leather-jacket man

looked very wholesome compared to these wraiths who hid from the sun and only went out at night to go clubbing. I had bumpkin status.

Fiona was living in a four-storey Georgian hovel in Carburton Street, behind Warren Street tube station, with an outside toilet that didn't have a roof. When a water pipe burst and flooded the cellar they'd used it as a swimming pool: 'We had a basement swimming pool once!' Her room was in stylish disarray, with fabulous dresses hanging from the picture rail, and stuffed full of dressing up – it seemed then that there were wonderful things to be discovered at jumble sales. Downstairs were Marilyn and Boy George. I don't know if they were lovers but they were sharing a room. Boy George was George then, a cheeky tearaway with his hair in ratty dreadlocks. It was post-punk so everyone had pseudonyms.

Next to the squat there was a derelict Lewis Leather shop in which Fiona decided to open a café called the Coffee Spoon, after T. S. Eliot's line, 'I have measured out my life with coffee spoons.' We broke into the building, discovering boots and pudding-basin crash helmets from the fifties – one of which I had for a while. We also found plaster models of christening fonts that we used as ashtrays, a very New Romantic-Goth touch. The Coffee Spoon had a repertoire of basic dishes, all named after poets. Toast was Robert Burns, beans on toast was Pam Ayres, and tea was T. S. Eliot. Jen painted a mural of a horse, there were Abba records playing and it was 10p for a plastic cup of cider. It was a word-of-mouth café where squatters in the area would come, pose and avoid sunlight. Pinkie Tessa sat around dressed as a lilac Little

Bo Peep with poke bonnet and arched eyebrows. She had a nipped-in waist because she had a corset on under her big skirt. Another squatter, Cerith, was incredibly tall, with greased-down hair and a big black overcoat. He had very long fingers like Aubrey Beardsley. All summer I hung out at the café, meeting pallid people dressed in black – I was struck by how pale everyone was. Everybody was hiding from the sun because New Romanticism and tan didn't go together.

I had thought I was the bee's knees in Portsmouth in my wacky clothes and felt secure in my position as one of the hip students there. I didn't like these art students in the café because they put my nose out of joint: they were cooler and worldlier, at ease in big London, whereas 'I were like from downe Portsmouth waye and I were only just getting used to that'. I had that cocksure teenage attitude of 'I know everything', then all of a sudden discovering I knew nothing. I was a yokel in bohemia.

Jen and I divided the people in the Coffee Spoon into Mods and Rockers. Mods were elegant, followed fashion, did the right thing, were neat, never messy. Rockers let it all hang out, made a mess, fell over drunk, weren't scared of making fools of themselves and took risks. Extrapolated, it was Classicism versus Romanticism. Most of the people that summer seemed Mod, especially the camp, gay boys. I thought gayness was, by definition, a Mod, over-scrubbed state whereas heterosexual was definitely Rocker.

There were occasional cabaret evenings at the café, where we took it in turns to put on a performance. John Maybury had been honing his film-making skills while

141

befriending Derek Jarman and showed a Super-8 film of his pretty boyfriend dancing at Andrew Logan's studio while reflected in a cracked mirror. His other reel was of Fiona dancing. In the film she was running towards the camera and at the exact moment she actually burst through the paper screen dressed in the same clothes.

The evening came for Jen and me to do our cabaret. For some reason Jen was crying as I was getting ready in Marilyn's room, so Marilyn came up to her asking, 'Is it because your boyfriend's a trannie, Jen?' and Jen burst out laughing. I thought she did have some awkwardness around my transvestism but perhaps that was caught from me. I was very uncomfortable with dressing up because it was the first time I was doing it 'out'. People were watching me because I had told everybody I was an official trannie. It was the first time I had got dressed in women's clothing in front of other people and when I was putting on a pair of tights one of the girls remarked, 'Oh, you've done *that* before!' because I was putting them on in the correct way.

I dressed as the cook, Fanny Craddock; Jen was in biker gear as Johnny, Fanny Craddock's husband. We were on my Suzuki 125. It was a stormy evening, the wind flung open the door, there was a crack of lightning, the crowd exclaimed, 'OWWWW!' and I rode straight into the centre of the café, revving up the bike, skidding to a halt in the middle of the floor. Then we cooked banana flambé. It was a cookery demonstration on a Baby Belling and I passed the flambé round for the audience to taste. The whole time I was achingly embarrassed.

The reason Jen and I had come to London for that

summer was because I had tramp fear. I had a tight budget to survive on for term-time but hadn't accounted for the vacation. When the summer holiday arrived, I panicked, 'Where am I going to stay?' I couldn't go back home because the old man said he never wanted me in the house again. The first time I was aware of having tramp fear was that spring when I told Jen, 'I like it when the weather's good because, if I have to, it's easier to sleep rough.' I felt safer when the weather was warmer. Tramp fear was a constant nag because financially I existed so close to the edge: it was an anxiety that lived with me for many years afterwards.

My only option for the summer was to stay with a friend of a friend, Mo, work as a security guard at the

Me/Jen/Veronica, 1981

local sports centre and hang out with Fiona. When Jen and I arrived at Mo's, she was in the throes of giving a Scottish party with handsome gay boys in frilly white shirts and eccentric students in kilts, tartan, sashes and long white socks. Mo was sweet, with a black bob and turquoise eyes, a fashion student at St Martin's. She gave us the room at the front of the flat above a bookmaker on the Holloway Road, right at the junction where the articulated lorries change down a gear and I was never able to sleep a wink unless I was dying of exhaustion. For someone who'd lived in the country and then in a quiet place like Portsmouth, the flat was incredibly noisy. We ended up on a single bed in the bathroom, which was inordinately inconvenient, but at least I was able to nod off.

New Romanticism was ironic and funny to us but also innocent, because of our youth. People wore fancy dress in the street, dressing as pirates, highwaymen or poets, with an abundance of velvet, high boots and frilly shirts, and got shouted at all the time. To Fiona, the obvious thing to do with all these people who wore costumes was to put on a New Romantic Christmas panto. That summer we began our rehearsals. It was to be *The Snow Queen* because Fiona had a script written for her Girl Guides by one of the local Guide leaders. She somehow managed to hire the Notre Dame Hall off Leicester Square, for one night only, and sold tickets. I was going to revive my Fanny Craddock as well as being an extra in the forest. The Two Roberts were drag queens who ad libbed wittily. Little Robert was short, Big Robert was tall, willowy and blond, and went on to have a sex change. Fiona, in leder-

144

hosen, played Kay, the boy who gets the shard of glass in his eye; while Jen, in a proper dirndl, played the girl who rescues him. Galinda, being an ice maiden, was the Snow Queen; her German accent gave her the perfect Snow Queen voice. Everyone joined in. It must have been awful in some ways, but funny. That Christmas it played to a packed house.

The summer taught me that art wasn't a nine-to-five job. I had been thinking art was an activity that you *did*, not something you *were*. The people in the squats lived art all the time; they were as creative in their food, clothes, conversation, nightlife, parties – in their everything – as in their art. Somebody once said, 'You cook your sculpture and you eat your paintings.' Everything was constantly evaluated and played with. Everything was an opportunity to be imaginative.

18

'I COULDN'T FIND THE LIGHT SWITCH IN THE LOO'

The Beaumont Society were obsessed with anonymity since they thought transvestism would be every member's worst secret and the press would be desperate to infiltrate, to expose everyone's predilection. So when I wrote requesting to join, I received a letter stating 'You must be vetted'. Jen and I dressed normally, then biked to a restaurant in Southampton to meet the local organisers for my interview. I was expecting to meet glamorous, fully garbed T-girls, but instead two elderly gents hobbled in wearing blue polyester trouser suits, eyeshadow and wigs, and looking like little old ladies. They'd been on a yacht en femme all day on the Solent. 'We love sailing dressed up!' they announced jollily. One was a farmer; he was perfectly passable. I breezed through the inspection; all they wanted to know was if I was an authentic trannie and not a journalist, or insane.

The Beaumont Society was staid, if it's possible for a transvestite society to be staid. I subscribed to the

Beaumont Bulletin, which was like a Women's Institute newsletter complete with crossword, a few fashion tips and a black-and-white photo of somebody using their pen name and membership number: 'By Sonia, No. 1264'. And no mention of sex whatsoever. The logo was the yin-yang sign with 'BB' in the centre. Beaumont was after the Chevalier de Beaumont de Eon, a famous cross-dresser in the seventeenth century who spied on the Russian court dressed as a woman and is buried at St Pancras church.

I decided to go to a Beaumont Society meeting. I donned a vintage Art Deco dress in grey silk, although I no longer needed a wig because I'd been growing my hair since I'd come out so it was fairly long, certainly long enough to be convincingly female. I put my goggles on over my badly applied mascara and chugged to Southampton. Jen came with me – by then she had christened transvestism the man-lady phenomenon. As we pulled up, I noticed a Mini parked in the street rocking because someone was getting changed inside. I thought, 'I bet we see him later.'

The restaurant was owned by one of the transvestites, who had closed it for the Beaumont Society function. There were a dozen men, one of whom was in his nineties and had been a pilot in the First World War. He staggered in, escorted by two helpers, wearing hugely high heels, a skin-tight satin dress over a corset and the most enormous loop earrings. He was the first person I'd seen with a pierced septum; he had a large gold ring through his nose. He talked very loudly, probably because he was deaf, about flying biplanes in 1917. There was Deborah, a glam cross-dresser who ran a bookshop and looked like a presenter from daytime television. I got on well with her and she came to Jen's degree show dressed up, and everyone thought she was my aunty. You refer to transvestites as 'she', it's polite.

We were sitting around dolled up when one member, a travelling salesman who used to dress in his campervan, then troll round the campsite at night, commented, 'I'm so jealous of you lot all dolled up, I've got my ball gown in the campervan but I haven't got my wig.' The lady who owned the restaurant offered, 'I can lend you one.' This was great. He went to the toilet to change and when he came out he had his wig on back to front, and his lipstick and eyeshadow looked as if it had been drawn on by a five-year-old. He said querulously, 'I couldn't find the light switch in the loo.' It would have been very out of order to laugh. Deborah leaned over and whispered in a kindly way, 'Here, let me sort you out . . .' turning his wig round and licking the corner of her hanky to wipe his make-up.

It felt odd to be there. Suddenly I was confronted with, 'I'm one of them. I'm like that. I look as gawky, awkward and funny as these men.' When I was dressed up alone it was easier to maintain the fantasy that I was a glamorous woman; in my mind I could distort my own mirror image as much as I liked. When I gazed in the mirror cross-dressed, I only perceived the transformation in my appearance, how different I looked although – in reality – I looked more similar than different.

There was a touch of the self-help group to the Beaumont Society: everyone had the shared pain of being forced to cope with transvestism. Some hadn't begun to put on women's clothes until they were late middle-aged,

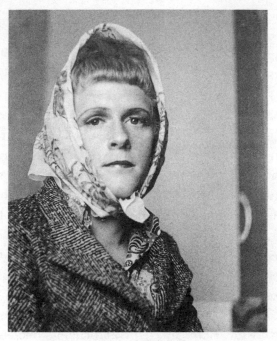
In the headscarf

one didn't start dressing until he was seventy – he suppressed it while he was married, waiting until his wife died. Most began cross-dressing when they were teenagers, some even younger. No matter at what age the men at the restaurant began dressing, none of them was fully passable as a woman. I learned that it is rare to meet a transvestite who is convincing; most aren't credible, they are blokes in dresses with wigs on. The stereotype is a man in his fifties in old-fashioned women's clothes, perhaps a knife-pleated skirt with tan tights. Trannies are part-timers, they're amateurs, although a posse of younger T-girls are emerging who are groovy and sexy.

Some, though very few, transvestites do transform

completely, and the mark of status in the Beaumont Society and the transvestite world is who looks most like a woman. The trannies of whom others comment, 'She's good! Look! You would *never* know,' are the leaders in a group. Trannies spot trannies. When I come across a transvestite I recognise her: I'm an expert, I've been doing it for thirty years. I'm alert to the smallest nuances, even in a realistic cross-dresser, because those are the nuances I scour myself for in order to eradicate them. The usual trannie look in public is furtiveness; moreover, trannies tend to have an air of excitement to them. Body language is the hardest aspect to suppress, facial expressions, rhythms and slight movements are gender different: men move with a muscularity and stiffness, women are more graceful. A wig invariably looks like false hair so having your own hair is a benefit. The most passable transvestites are small, old and need hardly any make-up. If I could change one aspect of my appearance I would choose to be shorter; being petite would help me look more androgynous and make it easier for me to pass as a woman.

There are blokes who arrive at a Beaumont Society weekend with four suitcases of clothes and five ball gowns, and constantly change their outfits throughout the following two days. Part of being a transvestite is having umpteen outfits and constantly acquiring lovely new clothes, sometimes lavish ones. Cross-dressers always have two wardrobes, perhaps having only one pair of jeans and four T-shirts for their male wardrobe but bankrupting themselves over their female closet. False bosoms and wigs can be costly too. A trans-gendered man will willingly pay considerable sums for elaborately embroidered garments, luxurious fabrics or custom-made clothing. Preciousness, display and ostentation are desirable. Trannies are usually too dressy, walking around on a weekday in clothes most women would wear to a wedding. It's because there's a tug between needing to look realistic but wanting to wear exhibitionistic clothes that express the feminine feelings – the frillies and the sexies. I've succumbed to the frillies and the sexies now because I'm no longer concerned about looking authentic. Transvestism is not about being a woman; it's about dressing as a woman.

When I'm dressed as a woman, I would never speak in a squeaky voice and defer to boorish men! I was once at a Beaumont Society trannie do in a pub function room in Twickenham. After the pub had closed a few select punters – ones who could be trusted not to cause any hassle – were let in so they could have a drink after hours. There was one bloke, a rugger-bugger type, who was boring on. After a while he said to us, 'I think you're amazing, I think you're brilliant because I find myself treating you like real women.'

I replied, 'Yeah, you've monopolised the conversation and ignored us. That's pretty realistic!'

I'll definitely be a transvestite for the rest of my life. It is agreed that transvestism in a man doesn't vanish. Many older trannies go full time, especially when they reach retirement: they no longer work, they have free time, so they decide, 'I'll live as a woman for the rest of my life.' There are a lot of little old ladies out there who are actually little old men. They trundle down to the shops with their trolley baskets. 'At peace' is how many of them describe it.

19

I STARTED INTERACTING
WITH THE
LOCAL WILDLIFE

My lecturer, Darrell Viner, was intense; there was a noose hanging up in his office and he was the first person I'd met who'd had psychotherapy. At the start of my second year I said to him in a student way, 'Oh Darrell, I'm stuck, oh, oh . . . I don't know what to do . . .'

He responded, 'Go away. Write ten pages about yourself,' which I did. Then he ordered, 'Now make that into an artwork.' That was all he said, I don't think he even bothered to read the essay. *Transvestite Jet Pilots* was my formative work and the first movement towards the art I make now. It was a dressing table carved into a jet cockpit. On top were a brush, comb and mirror moulded from clay alongside dinky pots decorated with penises – I made caveman versions because my skills were crude – and in the bottom drawer were five photographs of me transforming from Michelangelo's *David* into a trannie. I surrounded it with a parachute painted with sunrays so it looked akin to an altarpiece, then stuck on plaster feet.

Transvestite Jet Pilots

Detail of *Transvestite Jet Pilots*; inside the drawer, *David* through to Claire

153

Helen Chadwick was a visiting lecturer; she thought *Transvestite Jet Pilots* was good. It was a mishmash but it had an energy to it which none of my previous work had had. Art was no longer something I did for the lecturers, nine to five. Now I wanted to make art about me.

I felt more sophisticated. I had lived a little, had an adventure during my summer in London. I'd cycled to the National Gallery to see a painting of Chatterton lying on his deathbed and decided 'I want a shirt like that', so my apparel became a flowing white shirt, leather waistcoat, leather jodhpurs, riding boots and blowzy hair. I wore that outfit every day in the second year. I probably stank.

For my second year at college Veronica, Jen and I rented a tiny two-bedroom flat in the centre of Portsmouth. The day we moved in I sat down on the bed and was overwhelmed by a wave of relief at the security of having, what seemed like for the first time in my life, my own front door. The moment I landed in our flat, where I felt I had permission to be fully myself, I flowered. Until that moment I had been suppressed; now elements of myself – my anger, my creativity, my transvestism – were erupting.

A craze for fancy dress parties spread through college. Veronica and Jen were experimenting with body painting, so when we were invited to a gold party we decided 'Let's go painted gold'. We smeared baby oil on our bodies, then rubbed on gold powder, gilded ourselves *all* over, shrouded ourselves in cloaks, then sauntered to the party. I got very drunk and very rude. I went up to people and said what I thought of them, which was mainly negative. I was being horrible to everybody. I was naked and swinging from the banisters like an ape, yelling, 'You're all wankers! You're all wankers!' Eventually I became unbearable and they threw me out of the house. I had to scurry home in the nude, stained gold, cowering from shop doorway to shop doorway all the way to the flat. Fortunately Veronica was in when I got back.

To a white party I wore white: polyester hot pants, tight and sexy, a frilly see-through blouse, opaque tights and teetering PVC shoes with my hair in a beehive hairdo: I was inspired by Divine. A Hell's Angel was at the bash and when I glimpsed his bike – a Harley-Davidson, rare in 1981 – I blurted, 'Oh my God, my dream possession.'

At the end of the night I was tottering out of the party, inebriated, in my monochrome outfit when he asked, 'D'you wanna lift?'

I thought, 'Fucking hell! This is something!' as I sat on the back of his Harley, speeding down the street in my white hot pants.

For our Hallowe'en party we placed the bed in the middle of the sitting room, turned it into a rack and Veronica, in an all-in-one rubber bodysuit, tethered guests on to it. We had decided to re-create our own version of what we had experienced in London so every party had a theme: Robin Hood, Hollywood, Lurex. We had so many parties people became bored of coming to them. We had a party once where absolutely nobody turned up because we'd had three in the preceding fortnight. I've met people since who were scared of us, who said, 'You were so frightening at college.' I don't remember being alarming, but I suppose I was.

Seventy art students shared the college studio, which

was an open space with a zigzag of chipboard partitions and a Dancette record player that churned out a scratched collection of corny pop classics. Lou Reed and Nico featured. Each Friday we had to attend a Theoretical Studies tutorial. The lecturer, Sylvia Pringle, was blonde and bird-like, her skin was almost translucent and her hands were small and bony. She was a forty-three-year-old feminist in an olive-green boiler suit – twice my age exactly. I took to her, visiting her study for heart-to-hearts, finding her good to talk to because of her sympathetic ear: part of my general releasing was my need to communicate about my family and my past. She obviously read between the lines and realised I was a bit shop-soiled. Sylvia took me under her wing, encouraging me to read, write poetry and lent me books by modern poets: Craig Raine, Thom Gunn and rough blokes who wrote about this and that. In the spring of 1981 I was leaving her study after our chat when suddenly she grabbed me. I was utterly taken aback because she was my tutor. I wasn't accomplished at reading the signs from women nor do I remember thinking, 'I really fancy Sylvia,' but I was very keen nonetheless.

Jen had an inkling of what was happening, so I told her candidly, but I wasn't going to let Jen knowing stop me. I was also having sex every so often with the flatmate, Veronica. I was opening up. I was like a satellite landing on a foreign planet; all my solar panels opened, all my instruments went into operation and I started interacting with the local wildlife. I was naïve. I had let down my solar panels and I was fucking around; I was taking soil samples from Planet Earth.

Despite this I was very happy with Jen. We had a shared sense of fun and style but love wasn't part of my lexicon. I had a temper; if I was unhappy about something I could certainly let rip and shout, and Jen and I had a few set-tos. During long walks with her I began to see what I wanted from my life when we spoke about our hopes and dreams for our futures. We were both serious about becoming artists.

Simultaneously, my transvestism was flourishing; I had come out at college, had collated a woman's wardrobe and was occasionally togging up. After seeing a trick photograph of a Victorian drag queen marrying himself in Peter Ackroyd's *Dressing Up*, I bought a wedding dress and, with the assistance of the photography department, took a wedding photograph of me marrying myself. I was becoming more confident at going out dressed up as a woman until late one night when Jen, Veronica and I were ambling home from the Students Union disco. Normally when strangers were close by I was vigilant about not speaking because my voice would expose me. I can't have noticed that a gang of skinheads were trooping past. They bellowed, '*Thatsafella!*' Six skinheads, teenagers, began following us; I thought being with two girls when I was dressed up would protect me. For half a mile they were ten yards behind us chucking beer cans, baying, '*Cant! Cant!*'

We panicked: 'What are we going to do? Where are we going to go? We don't want them following us back to our flat and knowing where we live.' Just then a bigger, beefier skinhead joined them so we thought, 'Oh, fuck, here we go . . .'

He strode up to us and interrogated us, but in an intrigued, curious way: 'What's all this about then? Why are you dressed up?'

I was honest: 'We've been to the Students Union disco. This is my flatmate. This is my girlfriend.'

He commented, 'Oh, that's interesting,' then steered the other skinheads away. So we were rescued.

A couple of months later I walked along the high street in a lilac bridesmaid dress holding hands with a boy at college called John Potts. It was a balmy summer's evening and the football ground opened up as we passed; thousands of supporters swarmed around us but no one troubled us because they didn't realise. John Potts was gay, posh and poor, which was a funny combination, and wrestling with his homosexuality. He was very friendly with Veronica – Jen and I often wondered, 'Are they boyfriend and girlfriend?' I liked John Potts a lot, we were friends, he was quirky and a fine painter, sometimes we even slept together in the same bed. We didn't have sex but he used to ask me for a hug. I would think 'he is such a sweet chap' and he was very vulnerable too, so I'd let him cuddle me in bed.

I composed the ditty 'Captain Potts, Captain Potts, Wot is it wot you've got? You've got a lot' for my first attempt at film-making. John Potts and Veronica in their New Romantic costumes were star-crossed lovers and Jen, in my wedding dress, was an evil fairy who tears them asunder. I had a Standard-8 camera I'd bought from a jumble sale for one pound; Standard-8 was the 1950s pre-runner of Super-8. I had showed my camera to the film tutor who offered, 'I've got a reel of film to fit that. You can have it. It's been in my fridge for ten years.' I sent the reel to be developed and the company wrote back, 'This is an exceptionally old film that we no longer handle in England. It has been sent to Kodak in America to be processed.' When it returned the film was in an orange-blue hue with a blurred ghostly atmosphere that appealed to me and I wanted to do more film-making. I made another one when I visited my mum and stepfather in the New Year of 1983. My brothers were cast as two soldiers who were travelling up a river on a boat when they fell foul of a tribal woman who overpowers them and stings them into submission by blowing them kisses. It was based on *Apocalypse Now* and I called it *A Pucker-lipped Cow*.

20

'WE'VE GOT TO GO SOMEWHERE NICE WHILE WE'RE ON ACID'

The sole reason I was allowed to move into the squat was because I had a cooker. There wasn't a bedroom for me so I was put in the sitting room, which everybody went through to get to the kitchen, but I had a cooker and they didn't. The squatters didn't want a cooker to cook on but to do Hot Knives, which was when they put a blob of cannabis resin between two knives that they'd heated on my cooker and inhaled the smoke through a bottomless milk bottle. It gave them an instant high, far stronger and more hallucinatory than if they had smoked the dope. While they did Hot Knives, I would watch telly, waiting for them to go to bed eventually before I could go to sleep on the sofa. All evening there were endless cries of 'Where's the dope? Lost the dope!' followed by hysterical scrabbling about on the greasy carpet. I had the lowest tolerance of chaos so was constantly tidying the kitchen and sitting room, and couldn't keep any food – even a box of cornflakes – in the kitchen because the next morning it would be eaten. It used to drive me up the wall. One night I was on the sofa eating my beans on toast when a boy came in and jacked up in front of me. I thought, 'Do you have to do that while I am having my tea? It's not very nice.'

Going from the security of living with Jen and Veronica to, within a year, being back in an unstable environment was a low point, but I wasn't good at helping myself. Jen and Veronica were a year older than me, so by my third year they had graduated. Besides, I'd realised squatting had its advantages because I saved money on the rent.

I didn't know anything about drugs at all; I hadn't even smoked a joint when I moved into this seedy squat where everybody took everything on offer. I thought people who took drugs were boring because they just sat there having their own experience until my friend Danny took LSD and enthused about it. When I told this to Sylvia she just said, 'He's a fool,' because she had been young in the sixties and remembered it. She gave me Tom Wolfe's *Electric Kool-Aid Acid Test* about the original Merry Pranksters – the first people to take LSD as a leisure activity – in the hope I would think them all utterly stupid, but instead I thought, 'This is interesting.'

That Sunday afternoon Danny and I took half a tab. I was an acid virgin, so I didn't know what to expect. He said, 'We've got to go somewhere nice while we are on acid.' Two hours later I complained, 'Nothing's happening. It's got lost in my stomach. I can't see how a minuscule piece of paper can have any effect whatsoever.'

I was eating a cake in the café at the top of Butts Hill looking at the panoramic view of Portsmouth, when

Danny asked, 'You sure that acid isn't working?'

'No,' I insisted.

He said, 'Well, you're taking a bloody long time to eat that Eccles cake.'

Suddenly my mouth was crammed with broken seashells. I was extraordinarily aware of the shape and texture of every morsel of food on my tongue. I got a surge of paranoia because a child in the café was reading my mind, telepathically telling me, 'You're a DRUGGIE.'

'Listen to this,' Danny suggested. I put on his Walkman headphones and listened to Joy Division – one of those miserable doom bands – and it was the best music I had ever heard. I was transfixed. The trees began to sway in time with the music, the clouds started to flow in time with the music. Previously I hadn't been enthusiastic about music, now I instantaneously adored it. The trip didn't last long but it opened my eyes to drugs. I decided, 'That was intensely exciting. Brilliant-looking too.'

Danny and I went to the Headless Woman, a grim pub on the top floor of a multi-storey car park, to get some more acid. For two pounds we bought microdots; lentil-sized pillules adhered between two strips of Sellotape, like caps in a row. There was no bar code; the drugs could have been anything.

I took acid ten times, the most memorable being on May Bank Holiday in 1982. Twelve of us, including Jen, Veronica and Fiona – which added to the emotional frisson of the day – took the ferry to the Isle of Wight. We dropped the acid as soon as we arrived, then strolled along the seafront in the scorching heat, encountering the initial tingles. When we came to a private road with a toll-gate

Raymond, a beautiful black boy from the squat in London, lifted up the toll-gate shouting, 'We're going in. Here we go!' then dropped the barrier down behind us, stating, 'You're all in it now.' At the pinnacle of the trip I didn't know who I was, where I was, which way was up, which way was down, even whether I was human. I had no sense of time: ten minutes seemed like three hours, three hours seemed like ten minutes, time stretched elastically or evaporated. It was as scary as hell.

Jen was gripping on to a bush, convinced she was a leaf. She had a blank stare and wide, unblinking eyes. When we came to a gateway she was like a stubborn horse, she would not go through it so we had to push her urging, 'Come on, Jen! Come on!' My fear about Jen gave my paranoia something to focus on: I was screaming, 'Oh God! We've made Jen go *mad*!' The acid was far stronger than any of us had taken before. I had a silky halter-neck on, flowing hippy clothes and a handbag over my shoulder – I couldn't work out if I was a man or a woman. Raymond got sunburn blisters on the back of his neck and I asked him, 'Do black people get sunburn?' One girl from the year below me in college was lolling along with her skirt lifted up, rubbing her fanny. I kept wondering, 'Do people normally do that when they are walking along a country lane?'

The acid had made us thirsty and our mouths were parched. When we arrived at the seafront Fiona, being functional – or more functional than the rest of us – said, 'I'm going to get drinks.' She disappeared into a pub, emerging with twelve orange juices – she'd heard vitamin C in orange juice counteracts the effects of LSD. By now

Jen was catatonic on the beach, so Fiona began pouring juice into her mouth when, out of the blue, Jen gasped 'Oh!' in a 'Where am I?' way. Relief flooded through my body, like the drug itself: 'Jen hasn't gone mad!' From that moment on it was the funniest, weirdest, most brilliant day. Everything was unexpectedly exquisite, especially the reflections of the water on the sand.

That day is burned into my memory. It was one of the most disturbing things I have ever done: frightening, powerful and dangerous. My sanity and sense of being disintegrated, I didn't even know if I was alive or not. There were places I went into that were like dream states. I don't know if I'm glad or not that I had the experience.

Acid heightens everything including emotion. If I was in a dark mood I interpreted everything as an attack; if I was in a good state of mind everything was hilarious. If I was glum, everything became tragic. It wiped out my hard memories, leaving me with a soft, spongy memory: it was like taking a warm bath in all my recollections and feelings. The paranoia, the waves of paranoia, were incredible. When I look back on it, it was probably dangerous for me to take drugs with my emotional history. It's damaging, too. Psychotherapists used to prescribe patients LSD because they believed it would unlock repressed feelings, which it does, but in an exceptionally uncontrolled way. Jerry Garcia of The Grateful Dead replied, when he was asked if he still took LSD, 'It's like visiting Cleveland – if you've been there ten times you don't really need to go there again.' I visited Cleveland ten times and that was enough, it was kind of the same.

In my final year, artistically, LSD polluted my imagination. If my imagination and memory were a Rolodex,
one of those spinning wheels that sit on a desk with
addresses in it, acid was a Day-Glo highlighter so when
I was flicking though the Rolodex my eye was caught by
the Day-Glo highlighted ideas and I didn't notice anything
else. It forced certain images and styles to present themselves over and over again, and distracted me from the
natural flow of ideas arising in my imagination. I
embarked upon making objects cast in bronze that were
twee, olde-worldy, fiddly-diddly kitsch – acid-inspired art
tends to be sword and sorcery with a multitude of fluorescent pattern. I think of it as my Bilbo Baggins phase.

Celtic Crash Helmet, 1982. Celtic archaeology, motorbikes
and LSD – a heady brew

21

SOMETIMES WE WERE A BIT MORE ROBUST THAN THEY EXPECTED

The Death of Macho was the piece for my degree show that took the longest, was the least successful and marked me down. It was a figure of a classical god with a great big hard-on being crucified on a Harley-Davidson. Although it took many weeks of work to cast it in bronze, it was nevertheless twee. After it had come out of the mould I had this cast on my bench because I was working on it for my degree show and I was chiselling off all the flash – the extraneous bits – when we had a visit from the Arts Minister, Paul Channon. We were instructed to look very industrious while the Arts Minister was walking around the studio. As soon as he arrived I tore off a strip of emery paper and started polishing the knob furiously, shh-shsh, shh-shsh, shh-shsh, so when he came and looked over my shoulder I was wanking off this little sculpture as fast as I could with sparks flying.

I made *The Death of Macho* with the help of Derek, the foundry man who worked in the art department. I enjoyed working with the Derek and Derek liked working with me because I took the casting process seriously, doing it in the traditional way. Derek was a squat troll of a man with one eye because once metal had spat out of a cast into his other eye. The foundry was littered with snuffins because he constantly took snuff – I always knew where he'd been because there was a smelly, brown, powdery trail behind him. He said he was ex-SAS; he spoke about hitch-hiking on military aeroplanes across Europe to get home in time for Christmas.

For the degree show the chipboard jungle went up dividing the studio into spaces where students could put their exhibitions. I wanted a way of exhibiting my cast aluminium work that was self-contained. I constructed a giant's table, twelve feet long and six feet wide, from four massive charred railway sleepers that were lying in a pile by the railway line next to my squat. I nailed them together with eight-inch nails and displayed my degree show work on it. I got a 2:1, which was a representative mark because I had potential but, in the end, I didn't show it. I blame taking LSD.

The degree show was my first proper exhibition although only a few desultory people came because in Portsmouth there was hardly any art world. A feature of the show was the poor lost-looking parents who had never been down to the college before, wandering around bewilderedly: Mr and Mrs Beige Windcheater from Surbiton or Solihull, not quite knowing or understanding, thinking, 'God! Is this what our Jeffrey's been up to for the last three years!' My mother didn't visit my show but she came to my graduation with Uncle Eddie and his wife. I

Working on my degree show, 1982

Death of Macho: bronze figure

168

hired the gown and mortarboard, and we went through the ritual but it felt empty. Back at the squat I showed them my film of Captain Potts – I was very proud of it – by projecting it on to a blanket hanging over the window. I bought a lemon sponge cake and made cups of tea, which they found touching. My mother was horrified that I had orange boxes for chairs and blankets for curtains, but to me it seemed like perfectly normal student living, although there must have been a seediness to which I had become inured. I didn't know it then but my mother found it upsetting that I was living in squalor. I thought it was fine; it was how I'd lived for a year. By then I even had the master bedroom – the best bedroom in the squat.

While I was at college I had kept in contact with my mum on the phone maybe once a fortnight. I didn't see my dad very often; occasionally I visited him on the motorbike. All passion was spent in the relationship with my father. I still wanted my parents' approval. I don't think they understood my world. Perhaps they understand more, now that my mother has encountered it for herself. I don't know if it's true because I heard this third-hand, but my mother went into a local shop and the woman behind the counter was talking about her son who was a student at art college and who was obsessed with an artist called Grayson Perry, to which my mother responded, 'That's my son.' I don't know how believable that was. My mother was led through to the back of the shop where there was virtually a shrine to Grayson Perry. What must have gone through her mind?

The day after graduation, in July 1982, I hitched to Wapping with a mattress, a sleeping bag, a load of body paint and some ideas. For one week fifteen people were going to live in the nude in the B2 Gallery for a Neo-Naturist residency. The Neo-Naturists were Fiona, Jen and Angela, who had recently graduated in painting from St Martin's, along with a floating pool of people, of which I was one.

Angela sewed us each a bulky floor-length overcoat in fun fur, a material that was extremely unusual then, so we all had a fun-fur coat, which was useful for naked Neo-Naturists because they easily covered us, they were reasonably warm and they looked comical. Fiona visited the British Museum and, when no one was looking, did a quick flash while Angela took fantastic photos of Fiona standing naked next to Egyptian statues with a big face, like the Magritte painting, painted on her torso, before Fiona wrapped her cloak back round herself. Every lunchtime we would all put on our fun-fur coats and pop to the Prospect of Whitby pub and, of course, Angela's coat would fall open and the men who worked there used to love her, this woman with her tits falling out at the bar. They liked Angela so much that when they finished their lunchtime shift they would bring all the spare food from the Prospect round to the gallery and give it to us as a pretext for visiting Angela.

The gallery was beautiful, it had balconies – the old loading doors – that looked out on to the river and the weather was sunny all week. The audience were a small gathering of people who used to wander down to watch us while we were cooking or hanging out, but from noon onwards we would all be in the nude. We unfailingly got a good audience of dirty old men who came to stare at

Angela's bosom, because Angela had huge breasts and a very slim model figure.

The first day's theme – every day had to have a theme – was Art Day, so Fiona invited every artist she knew to come to the B2 Gallery to use our bodies as canvases. Andrew Logan, Dougie Fields and even Derek Jarman came, and we stood around while the artists painted us. Paint was flicked on Angela with a toothbrush until she was like a Jackson Pollock painting. In the evening we had a private view where we posed motionless, being the art. Macbeth Day had an evening performance of the play although it was an extremely fleeting version of *Macbeth*, ten minutes long, with seven witches because they were the favourite part. Fiona was Mrs Macbeth: she had an industrial cooker on stage and spent most of her perform-ance draped in tartan, frying Scottish pancakes. I was the Forest of Dunsinane, holding up a bundle of buddleia that I'd ripped up from an old East End bombsite, and covered in body paint that was mixed with Scottish oats so I had a crusty tree trunk texture all over me. The porridge set hard in the same way that when cereal sticks to a bowl it turns rock hard, clinging to the hairs on my body some-thing chronic. This crusty oatmeal was *all* over me. It was very, very painful to move in, let alone wash off. After our performance we were directed to sprint out of the gallery screaming, so I hobbled down the road feeling quite vulnerable.

Fashion designers painted us on Fashion Day for an evening catwalk show during which we modelled body-painted clothes. The fourth day was Black Day where we were only allowed to use black body paint. It was the most photogenic day. There were people in stripes, splatters, dots and tribal markings, all these adults of varying body shapes in various patterns. At the Black Picnic we sat in the nude on Wapping beach eating solely black food – black bread, black pudding, black olives and Guinness. We looked like a strange, apocalyptic tribal gathering. A police boat chugged past and juddered to a halt when it spotted us.

The Black Day picnic, Wapping

By the fifth day we were all manky. Bath time was a massive chore because there were fifteen Neo-Naturists yet only enough hot water for one bath. So if I was fifteenth into the bath it wasn't very enjoyable. I was lucky even to get the body-paint off me. By Punk Day all my crevices had collections of brightly coloured dirt in them. Word had passed around about our installation so a big crowd arrived for a heaving Punk Day party. Everyone was sniffing glue as a punk homage – someone had turned up with a gigantic tub of Evostick – and getting halluci-natory. I wasn't sniffing glue, it didn't appeal to me; instead, I made a very raw video of the night.

The week ended. I had left college and I was very fright-ened because I didn't know what the hell was going to happen. I had applied for an extension on the unreality that is student life. I had an interview at Chelsea School of Art to do an MA in sculpture, but they rejected me because they said I had too strong a voice, was too much of an artist and not enough of a student. Jen and I decided we must move to London because that was where every-thing was happening. We heard that the basement of Marilyn's squat, a big house in Crowndale Road next door to Camden Palace, was empty. Marilyn was becom-ing a pop star, although he was already taking heroin, and there were a couple of other junkies in the squat and I think the woman on the top flat was a prostitute. Nobody wanted the basement of the house because it had been flooded and had a fire so it was both very damp and very black. An elderly Irishman had abandoned it, leaving it littered with empty beer bottles, Catholic regalia, medals and, sadly, whole drawers full of birthday cards from the previous thirty years. Jen and I clambered in through the window and saw that the basement was horrendous but we were desperate as we had nowhere to live. I knew how to rig up the electricity so we turned on the electric fires in every room to dry the flat out and we put the soggy mattress next to a fire to dry. Apart from hot water the flat had everything we needed and it was free, nor were we afeared of being evicted because the council realised that squatters kept derelict properties in better condition than if they were left empty to rot. I didn't particularly like living in the same house as a lot of junkies, though, because they kept nearly dying.

Jen was a good homemaker and I took great pride in the decoration. The walls had originally been pastel pink, but despite our spending days scrubbing them they remained half sooty black and dusty especially in the corners, which gave the decor a trendy, distressed look. All our furniture was from skips, as were the stinky carpets. I made a throne from scaffolding boards. We had drapes, posters, pictures, pieces of jewellery and Jen's paintings hanging up on the dusky walls. It was Gothic. No matter how rough the flat was – there were mushrooms growing in a damp patch in the hallway where the water heater dripped – we had a base, we felt secure. It was exciting. That first night, after we had dried the mattress out enough, we squeezed into the cell-like bedroom which backed on to the car park of the Post Office sorting office and it was noisy all night long with banging doors and shouting postmen, but it was a home and that was enough.

The unofficial grant for artists was the dole with its depressing experience of signing on – perpetual queuing in rooms cluttered with horrible nylon-covered chairs. I lost my dole money once, the whole £28, on the way home from cashing the cheque, that was depressing too. The dole wasn't enough to live on but what appealed about poverty was that it removed all my decisions. I had no spare money, so I didn't have to consider what to spend it on; there was a relaxation to that. I only bought food

– the cheapest food – and I got clothes when we had a few extra pence to go to a jumble sale. There was no money at all for luxuries. To get some cash we did life modelling in art colleges, standing in the nude getting very bored and stiff. It's hard work sitting still. I realised that when I was naked in the class, people would be scared of me and slightly back away. I never saw a good drawing of me in all the time I did it.

In the spring of 1981 Fiona met a tightrope walker. Hermine was married to the poet Hugo Williams and had scripted *Sheherazade*, a feminist version of *The Tales of a Thousand and One Nights*, which Fiona and Hermine decided to stage. Fiona was Sheherazade, Raymond was going to be the sultan – the main male lead – and everyone was cast in some part or other. We didn't have to bother with costumes because it was going to be a Neo-Naturist production. I volunteered to do the set, but had no materials whatsoever. Lying around the squat I found several piles of rotting carpets that I painted skulls and tribal patterns on to with old household paint, then hung them up as the backdrop. I assembled all the household furniture we didn't want in the flat, nailing offcuts of wood into it to construct thrones and altarpieces. We did our second Neo-Naturist performance at the Notre Dame Church Hall again, although this time we did two performances. People bought tickets and it was a well-attended production, with an assemblage of nude actors, featuring in a Sunday tabloid under the headline KIDS IN NUDE ROMP IN CATHOLIC CHURCH HALL.

On the success of the show we were booked to do a Neo-Naturist performance in Brixton at the Spanish

Neo-naturist show

Anarchists Association, which was similar to a working men's club, an extremely anachronistic place that had become somewhat hip because of punk's associations with anarchy. As it was May Fiona thought we should do a Communist, May Day-themed cabaret. Cerith, Fiona, Jen, Angela and I all had identical Communist uniforms body painted on to us with khaki paint and we decorated ourselves with big red five-pointed stars. We spent that afternoon making placards with very naïvely drawn self-portraits with joke Chinese versions of our names underneath, like Gray-SUN, Jen-Bin and ANG-lee-AI, which we nailed on to wooden poles. Cerith was going to give a reading from Chairman Mao's *Little Red Book* and we had a record of the Red Army Choir to play. We had what Fiona decided were capitalist consumer objects, little pottery knick-knacks that we were going to smash.

The performance consisted of us goose-stepping into the room to the strains of the Red Army Choir, reading from the *Little Red Book*, smashing the capitalist consumer artefacts, making pseudo-political gestures and declarations, then marching around while waving our placards. It only lasted ten minutes. We were cavorting and having a very good time, with no political message involved, but when we goose-stepped out of the room at the end of the record there was a dead silence. There were around a hundred anarchists in the audience as well as some punks and they all hated it, not one of them clapped, the room was dead quiet. The only sound was of us laughing in the men's toilets, these echoy, chipped urinals, wondering, 'What have we done?'

We all piled into a taxi, painted and naked, then did the same performance at the Fridge nightclub round the corner, in exchange for free entrance and drinks. The performance received a very antagonistic response at the Fridge, mainly because of me, a man, being naked. A bloke in the audience had encouraged his girlfriend to climb on stage and grab my willy when suddenly there was the sound of smashing glass and a guy with a broken beer bottle clambered on to the stage. We were standing there, scared stiff in the nude. The bouncers leapt on stage and shoved us off halfway through our performance. It was a real kerfuffle. We were innocents, we had thought our show was fun but the drunken, aggressive blokes did not like it. When men were performing as Neo-Naturists it was edgier because then the show couldn't be about titillation; instead, it mocked the concept of titillation because we were unselfconsciously nude, we weren't glamour models, nor were we necessarily fantastic physical specimens. The performance implied, 'Right now you should be seeing naked cabaret performers in tutus, boas and itsy-bitsy tassels but instead you've got us lot. You've got a bunch of pseudo-hippies prancing about doing performance art and being a bit boring, actually.' There were various provocative dissatisfactions involved that I think caused the hostile reaction, though sometimes at gay clubs, like Heaven, we would get a fantastic reception.

Jen and I did our own Neo-Naturist performance at the Camden Palace where I was a painter in a smock and beret while Jen was my canvas. We were placed in the foyer as people were coming in. I don't think the management knew what they were letting themselves in for, as we were a bit more robust than they expected. I was painting a Picasso on to a naked Jen, all very innocent. Then I took all my clothes off. We had a great big French stick and two bread rolls sellotaped together which Jen sellotaped on to me like a big willy. Then Jen got out a bread knife and was cutting off slices of my willy. She also had a whip that she was dipping into green paint and was whipping me with while people were coming into the club and buying their tickets. We got hustled off when we did that, it got a bit too much for the management.

We gave a lot of probably quite tedious Neo-Naturist performances where the audience would be shouting, 'Get them on! Get them on!' We did poetry, very bad gymnastics, maypole dancing and all the girls gave birth on stage in puddles of blood. On nights when we weren't doing Neo-Naturist performances we went clubbing at places

'Famous Five': Jen and Grayson off to Ardnamurchan

with free entry. I used to go to the Taboo nightclub in a black suit with skin-tight Lycra trousers and a jacket two sizes too small – so it was very tight – and a naff shirt and tie. I put sunburn-coloured make-up on my face and left white rings round my eyes, like ski goggle marks. I wore steel-capped shoes and big sunglasses. And I had a tail. It was a stiff, furry dog's tail, like one of those that hits you round the leg. I hooked it on the back of my belt and there was a hole in the back of my trousers where it poked out. That year there was a photo of me wearing that outfit in *Harpers and Queen* for an article called 'English Eccentrics'. In the article I describe myself as poet, film-maker and artist. Pretentious twit! I don't think the word transvestite even cropped up because that was still very much a quiet thing.

I separated my transvestism from my social life because

Claire in a photo-booth at Euston station, 1983

I was into male fashions at the time. Claire was something I did in the daytime on my own, though Claire was blossoming because I felt stable and London seemed to be a reasonably tolerant society, so she kept coming out of the woodwork. I found a stall at Brixton market that sold oversized women's shoes and bought a pair of slingback sandals. I dressed up and trolled to Oxford Street in the daytime, and occasionally to an opening, wearing a hippy dress that I liked very much, a floaty frock from the late seventies. By then my hair was long, thick and curly. I thought I looked like an off-duty nurse or an Avon lady and took photographs of myself in the photo booth at Euston station. I would skulk down to the West End on my own, travelling by tube dressed up, despite the underground having the most unflattering lighting and being trapped in a carriage with anybody who might hassle me. If I had been confident about dressing as a woman, people would have treated me like a woman but because I was uncomfortable and inexperienced within myself, people didn't know how to deal with me. In my early twenties I was not wholly accepting of myself. I was nervous and still ashamed of cross-dressing; it would be a long time before I would be able fully to embrace my sexuality and publicly celebrate Claire.

22

POTTERY AND
NIGHTCLUBS AREN'T
EASY BEDFELLOWS

My first proper pottery lesson was in September 1983.
Fiona went to pottery evening classes at the Central
Institute. She said, 'The teacher's really nice. You should
come along, Grayson.'

I wanted to be an artist, to get a gallery and an exhibition. I had been working hard at making small sculptures on our kitchen table, building pieces from junk I'd
found on the pavements or in skips around the squat. I
built Baba Yaga's hut – Baba Yaga was a witch in a Russian
fairy tale that ate children, flew about in a pestle and
mortar, and lived in a hut balanced on chicken legs. I
bought a chicken, hacked its feet off, dried them in the
oven, then varnished them. I made the hut to fit the
chicken's feet, which set the scale, then we ate the chicken.
I also made a tower out of tiny flints stuck together with
plaster and Polyfilla. Every day I was working intensely
on the elaborate collages in my sketchbook for which I
had a colossal collection of encyclopaedias, textbooks and

old World War One tomes I'd accrued from jumble sales. I spent hours pouring over and cutting up these books while a record played in the background. The collages' obsessive detail, busyness and horror vacui set the tone for the work I make now: even if it is a pot that doesn't have an image on it, it has to have a texture; it has to have marbling or crackle. I find it difficult to leave empty space, my instinct is to cover up emptiness and always elaborate, to my detriment sometimes. It's part of my psychological make-up that I'm a detail freak.

I had made things at college with clay, buggering about, but not *learned* about pottery. Clay was a material I could mould; it didn't have anything to do with ceramics in the classical sense. I had used clay as if it were Plasticine, then hoped the sculpture would survive in the kiln; very rudimentary sculptures which, more often than not, would come out badly.

The teacher at the evening classes, Sarah Sanderson, had all the attributes of a classical pottery teacher: she wore patterned trousers and liked all things Japanese. A self-confessed tea snob, she always brewed her own cup of tea at break rather than drink tea from the canteen. She was a very competent thrower who threw small porcelain pieces and she was a good teacher in that she took command of the class as well as giving clear instructions. I was hard-working, but at the same time I wanted to get on with my own work independently. She would give me advice about how to get what I wanted or I would pick up things from overhearing what she was telling other people. This was the first time I had been exposed to proper lessons, pottery skills and traditional techniques

AUSTRIA·HUNGAR
QUAINT PEA

Home of a Peasant

The Burden Bearers

Collage, 1983.

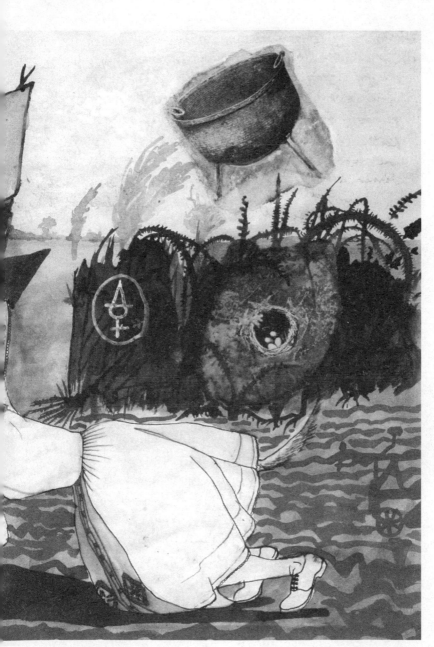

'Baba Yaga's Hut'

like coiling, glazing, stencilling, all of which I now use. The first thing I made was a devil giving birth. I'd embedded fragments of glass in it, which melted. That got stolen.

I went to classes once a week to begin with but enjoyed it so much that I wanted to do more. First it was Thursdays, then Wednesdays as well and then I started going to the Friday daytime class because on Fridays there was no teacher so I could do my own work undisturbed. I only paid £1 per lesson because I was on the dole.

It was around this time that, according to my mother, my stepfather had an affair with someone on his paper round at the American Air Base and my mother decided she wanted a divorce. I was urging her, 'Yeah, go for it!' She told me all about it during our fortnightly phone calls. My stepfather apparently got down on bended knee and declared his undying love and, I think, need. He had a romantic vision of them going away and having a lovely new start so they sold the big Barrett house in Great Bardfield and bought a dairy farm in Scotland – I got roped in to driving the removal lorry. As soon as we had unloaded the lorry my youngest brother, who was twelve, was being taught how to look after a dairy herd. It was disastrous; milk prices dropped, then they were hit by mad cow disease.

When I returned to London after helping my mum and stepfather move, I went to the V&A to look at ceramics – I hadn't looked at ceramics properly before and the V&A had a vast collection. It was a treasure trove and I was very inspired by it, particularly the slipware dishes by Thomas Toft. Slipware is traditional English earthenware, usually in earthy colours – brown, white, black, beige – and the decoration is done with liquid clay, which is almost like icing. Some of the earliest decorative ware dates from the seventeenth and even sixteenth centuries, and they are very prized now. Thomas Toft, who died in 1689, made large meat plates called chargers, decorated with coats of arms, Charles I or a bloke on a horse, very free and naïve because they were drawn with a slip trailer. Slip trailing had been a traditional technique in pottery and this was the period when it was refined. Toft was the most famous because his were the most elaborate and accomplished chargers; they were big, about fifty centimetres in diameter, naïve, but fun pieces that would have been hung on the wall. There was a certain old-worldly half-timbered pubness about his work that I liked. After looking at the old English slipware in the V&A I made a sculpture of a boar.

We'd had a history teacher at school who was a naval type with a twiddly beard and moustache, and at the end of one term he said 'I'll give you a treat', so he read us some salacious stories out of history. One story was about King James, the gay one. When the king and his men went hunting and caught the deer, they would slit open the deer's stomach so all the guts would pour out, then the king would take off his shoes and breeches, and waddle about in the intestines: he'd get turned on by this, it was a fetish of the king's and that interested me. So I made this little figure of the king cavorting inside the belly of a boar in Ye Olde English Pottery.

I learned that you could place certain materials on the clay and they would melt very uncontrollably in the kiln so I put some pieces of glass on the figurine that oozed into the clay. I had a huge collection of coloured glass from Portsmouth beach, which was covered in sea-worn glass from a Victorian rubbish dump, and I used to mudlark by the Thames for chips of pottery, splinters of glass and interestingly shaped pieces of metal that I'd incorporate into the sculptures.

My initial frustration was that everything in pottery takes a long time, with a lot of waiting around for things to dry. I would be working on a piece when I'd get to a point where I couldn't do any more because it would need to dry, so I always needed to be working on two or three projects simultaneously. Very soon I was producing two or three pieces a week. Everybody else produced two or three pieces a term.

In those early lessons I was being provocative, I was an angry young man, I wanted to offend so I was using the rudest images I could think of: women being shagged by wolves, handicapped Fascists, Thalidomide girls, lots of swastikas, S & M hospitals, all the stuff that was free-flowing very crudely out of my mind. The other people in the class were a mixed bunch and I always thought no one was taking any notice of what I was putting on my pots. Apparently some students led a delegation to the head of the college to complain about me. To his credit the head said, 'Oh, leave him alone. Let him get on with it.'

Although all the most important elements of my future life were present, at the age of twenty-two I didn't know that pottery and pot making would become the central medium of my career and my exhibitions so far. A year into pottery classes I decided, 'Right, I've got to get an exhibition,' got together slides of my work and walked into a little gallery opposite the British Museum, showed the slides to the owner who put me in a mixed show in December 1983. What characterised the period from the evening classes until I was in my thirties, when I got married and my daughter came along, was that I lived life to the full in the here now, and didn't think too much about my past or my future. I did the things you do in your twenties: I went out, I got drunk, took a few drugs, had a lot of sex, and somehow I got a lot of pottery made as well. After seven years Jen and I split up – she put up with my affairs, then had one of her own and left me for someone else. I broke contact with my mother in 1990 when I went to visit taking my future wife, Phil, whom I met in evening classes. My mother attacked Phil and said, 'You must be desperate to marry a transvestite.' My childhood in Essex and the events described in this book would overshadow me until I went into therapy at the age of thirty-eight and Claire, who was always around, would then be able to blossom fully. Claire and her frocks would continue to crop up in my art; a lot of things that are part of my life appear in my art.

Some of the things I made when I was in my first year of pottery classes were bad. Often they would literally fall apart. I found the communal glaze firing frustrating – my work was never fired in optimal conditions, tending to be under-fired, which meant the glaze looked like semi-translucent snot. Some of the early pots have a horrible texture. They were failures. They were irredeemably ugly objects; either the glaze didn't turn transparent, or the colours were not what I intended. I would get work out of the kiln and the teacher would say, 'Shame it's cracked,' and I'd reply, 'Ah, but that's a genuine crack, that's not one of your pottery technique cracks. It's a genuine mistake by someone who really can't do pottery very well yet, and it is worth a dozen of your carefully contrived Japanese-style cracks.'

I often create pots difficult to make and am overambitious technically, contriving to make them very complex to balance. I deliberately don't do tests. I'm loath to try out new techniques by doing a maquette, a dummy run, because the second time I use it is never as good as the first. Instead, I try new techniques I've not used before – perhaps a combination of colour or a new transfer – on major pieces. It could go disastrously wrong and sometimes it does. Often I rescue a pot, usually with gold lustre. I bodge things over but they always scream 'bodged' to me and probably to other potters too. But bodged is OK because it is part of being human. I want an element of bodging in my work – I wouldn't want it to be calculatedly perfect. I want it to be slightly flawed. Sometimes I'm almost disappointed when things work exactly as I imagined.

I'm constantly searching for a balance between slightly clunky awkwardness and genuine sensuous beauty. I start a pot with an atmosphere, which is a combination of style, emotion and content. But the perfection I am after in my imagination, the fuzzy golden glow, can never exist. I want the pot to have a specific feeling but then I have to put that feeling into a material object that is subject to the whim of technique and practicality. Every time I open the kiln, there is an air of disappointment. Often

I open the kiln and hate the piece. It's the search for the perfect pot. It's the fight against the terrible cruelty of the material reality in the traumatic birth from my imagination. I'm not in love with my pots; I'm in love with the sensual beauty they can give.

I didn't really think pottery was my metier. I didn't suddenly switch and think, 'This is it.' It took me a long time, between ten to fifteen years after these lessons and almost thirty years after my very first pottery lesson at primary school, to realise that pottery was my prime medium. Even now it's up for grabs. I enjoy pottery but it's not as if I was born to do it. In ten years' time I could make vases as a sideline if something else came along that I was passionate about. At the moment I'm very excited about printmaking.

When I started pottery lessons I was more interested in film-making because I enjoyed making Super-8 films so much. Pottery was a funny dalliance that I did as a tease. I had no investment in it, which was a healthy position to be in as an artist. I had no preconceptions, no agenda; it was me mucking around at something I liked. I returned to my bedroom fantasy mentality of Alan Measles and his world while I was making things with clay. When I was a child growing up in rural Essex I didn't have any agenda over the many years I spent playing with Alan Measles and in pottery classes I didn't have any career agenda around ceramics. The searchlight of my career was pointing to film, which was fashionable and slotted in well with the trendy lifestyle I aspired to. Pottery was a joke. Pottery wasn't a glamorous proposition – it still isn't. Jen, Fiona and I aspired to glamour; we were emerging from New Romanticism. I went nightclubbing every night; pottery and nightclubs aren't easy bedfellows! I was interested in fashion and hanging out with groovy people. Working with clay was unhip, *really* uncool. I could only tolerate ceramics being square because of the nature of Jen and Fiona, and our raucous laughter about the notion of being fashionable. The self-conscious ridiculousness of being funky was all so funny. We always had a perspective about our aspirations.

I was attracted to pottery because it was naff; that was the subtext. I was aware of ceramics being the underdog

Kinky Sex, 1983

and that was one of its saving graces. It's very British; pottery will never become bad taste. It will always have that woody, nutty, wholesome, truth-to-materials-ness around it. It was never going to be a flashy, gay, window-dressing art, it was always going to be humpy, hetero-sexual and earthy. However trite and dilettante the images I put on the clay, the material would bring it, literally, down to earth. One of the great things about ceramics is it is not shocking so I thought, 'I can be as outrageous as I like here because the vice squad is never going to raid a pottery exhibition.'

I had seen the ceramics at the V&A, returned to the evening classes and asked the teacher, 'Have you got a plate mould? I'd like to make a plate.' The very first one worked reasonably well – because I put a coin over Jesus's cock it appeared as if he had had an enormous wet dream while being crucified. So I made my first ever plate, which was called, *Kinky Sex*.

Refugees from Childhood, 2001

ACKNOWLEDGEMENTS

Grayson Perry

Wendy Jones for being pure and unshockable, and for laughing at my offensive jokes. Rex Bradley for giving me back the deeds to my interior landscape. Phil, for her strength and love, and Flo for being Flo. Jen for seven precious years of youth together. Christine, for her creative energy. Mary and Arthur for solid love.

Wendy Jones

I would like wholeheartedly to thank the following people who, from the inception of the book, have encouraged and guided me, supported and taught me, even told me off on occasion. Leila Berg for being a safe haven for many years. Sarah Bylinski for babysitting. George Frankl for his astonishing mind and his love. Ruth Freeman for her reliability and wisdom. David Godwin and Sarah Savitt for doing business with panache on my behalf. Jane Monson for her purity and poetry. Julie and Colin for telling me stories about their childhoods. Mary Mike for her merry dance on a radical path. Grayson Perry for trusting me. Angela Price for gentle trustworthiness. Lorna Sage for ferocious teaching. Will Self for telling me, in no uncertain terms, which way was the wrong way. Clare Sims, my partner in crime in all things literary, for a lot of encouragement and savvy advice. Jenny Uglow for warm and incisive editing. Rob Allen for convincing me the Luddites were wrong, and for giving me joy, stability and Solly.

LIST OF ILLUSTRATIONS

Endpapers
Front: 'No Artist – Mother I am a fascist!'
Back: 'Mother visits the artist's studio'

Colour plates

Illustrations in the text